youth rugby
101 *drills*

Also available in the series from A & C Black

101 Youth Football Sessions
Tony Charles and Stuart Rook

101 Youth Fitness Drills – Age 7–11
John Shepherd and Mike Antoniades

101 Youth Fitness Drills – Age 12–16
John Shepherd and Mike Antoniades

101 Youth Cricket Drills – Age 12–16
Luke Sellers

chris sheryn
anna sheryn

youth rugby

101 *drills*

second edition

A & C Black • London

First published in 2006 by A & C Black Publishers Ltd,
this edition published by A & C Black, an imprint of
Bloomsbury Publishing PLC
36 Soho Square, London W1D 3QY
www.acblack.com

Second edition published 2011

ISBN: 978 1 40813078 0

A CIP catalogue record for this book is available from the British Library.

Note: It is always the responsibility of the individual to assess his or her own
fitness capability before participating in any training activity. While every effort
has been made to ensure the content of this book is as technically accurate as
possible, neither the author nor the publishers can accept responsibility for any
injury or loss sustained as a result of the use of this material.

Cover artwork © Tom Croft
Inside photographs: pp. viii, 21, 30, 43, 55, 63, 73, 83, 89, 94, 106, 116, 124, 129,
134 © Getty
Textual illustrations by Mark Silver

A & C Black uses paper produced with elemental chlorine-free pulp, harvested
from managed sustainable forests.

Typeset in 10/12pt DIN Regular by Margaret Brain, Wisbech, Cambridgeshire
Printed and bound in Great Britain by Martins the Printers

CONTENTS

ACKNOWLEDGEMENTS

This book is an amalgamation of ideas and experiences from a number of different coaches from both league and union codes. For their help with this project I would like to thank the following: David Jackson, for some inspirational ideas on introducing tackling and defence; Simon Scull, who has proven to be a great help on all areas, especially goal-kicking; particular thanks to Wyn Sheryn, who has been the fellow burner of midnight oil. Wyn has been coaching a range of ages and sports over the past 40 years – from schoolboys to Olympians. He is currently working in not-so-semi-retirement at Hutton Grammar School in Preston introducing 11-year-olds to the great game. It is from his work there with Alf Odie that many of these drills spring.

INTRODUCTION

This book is designed to provide group leaders with a resource to construct effective frameworks within which young players (under the age of 16) can develop the skills required for rugby union. The focus is on the *basic* skills and concepts that should be at the heart of any good player's game, and for this reason you will see an emphasis on the themes of movement and core passing and catching skills. Highly complex, advanced tactical drills have not been included as they are not appropriate for this age group.

Experiences in the important early years of life can determine whether or not children continue to play into adult life and can, in many cases, colour their view of sport in general. It is therefore important to remember that the key objective for any training session with children is to create an environment to which the players want to return. I hope that the drills and ideas in this book will help to produce sessions that are stimulating, productive and above all fun for all concerned, including you, their coach.

Fiona Pocock of England avoids one tackle and makes an attacking run with the ball during the Women's Rugby World Cup semi final against Australia in 2010.

SESSION GUIDELINES

Understanding the younger player

It is now generally accepted that pre-adolescent players require special handling and should not simply be treated as 'mini-adults'. For physiological as well as psychological reasons, training sessions must take account of the fact that children have different requirements.

It is important to remember that children will reach puberty at different ages – the chronological age for one adolescent may be up to five years out of sequence with a counterpart of the same age. It is therefore imperative that those organising group training sessions should not assume that all players are equal in physical ability or capacity.

Pre-adolescents

Generally speaking, pre-adolescent children are flexible and weak in relative terms. It is therefore not necessary to get them to do any formal flexibility work. They also are, by nature, aerobic animals. They have no anaerobic capacity so it is not appropriate for them to do any separate formal strengthening work.

However, their rugby 'technical' work should emphasise appropriate movement patterns which in themselves will have a strengthening effect, e.g. throwing activities to strengthen and teach appropriate patterns of movement. As it is an age where habits are learned, it is a good idea to encourage movements that will be used in later life.

Adolescents

Adolescents are generally the opposite to their younger counterparts in respect to their overall physical profile – they are relatively strong and inflexible. These characteristics will be more pronounced during growth spurts. Flexibility work is a good idea, and specific attention should be made to the hamstrings and calf muscles (especially during and just after growth spurts, when muscle length can lag behind increases in long bone length). Tightness in these muscle groups has been linked to episodes of anterior knee pain – especially common in adolescent girls.

For example

Demonstrating a skill with your back to another pitch with players running around will mean that your group will have varying degrees of focus on you. Be aware of what is going on behind you. If you are introducing young children to catching practice it is a good idea to ensure that the backdrop to the object ball is uncluttered, or at least as still as possible.

Appealing to the senses

Children can process information from several senses all at once, many of which can be used to enhance learning. Different children will place a different emphasis on each sense and you need to be aware of this when coaching a skill. For example – when teaching a player to kick a ball, consider:

- **Visual** – body shapes
- **Tactile** – how the ball feels on the foot at point of impact
- **Aural** – what sound is made when the skill is well executed

By asking the children to describe their own perception of the skill during practice, a coach can build an understanding of which learning strategies the players are using, and use this knowledge to better communicate.

For example

To ensure that the correct elements are retained for use in the drills following demonstration, the effective coach will emphasise the ONE coaching point, repeat it, demonstrate it, and then reinforce it so that when the group breaks up there is no doubt as to the element for practice.

How best to learn

Traditionally the teaching of a skill has been approached by simple repetition, in the understanding that practice makes perfect. However, research has shown that while some simple repetition for the complete beginner is beneficial, varied practice can provide faster and more permanent results.

For example, when teaching to throw into the lineout, faster progression can be made by varying the points to which the hooker is throwing – long, short, lobbed, flat, etc., rather than standing and aiming at a single point repeatedly.

It is thought that the extra return could be due to the requirement to constantly revisit and most importantly adapt, driving the skill to a deeper level of understanding. The fact that the player is being presented with different problems to solve means that the ability to adapt learned skills develops.

The learning curve

The development of a skill during a group practice will not follow a straight line. It is normal for awareness and concentration to be high initially, and for skills to develop accordingly. However, as the drill progresses, concentration levels will fall as will the accuracy of execution. If allowed to continue unchecked by the coach, competency levels will suffer.

To address this issue, coaches must constantly be aware of the pattern and take time to rest the players' minds and bodies. Stop the drill, re-communicate the objective and the skill and then once the players are rested and ready – both mentally and physically – start again. In this way the inevitable decline in competency can be halted, and the development curve can edge upwards once again.

It is important that children are taught to adapt the skills that they have learned, like these youngsters playing in the then-Powergen Cup Final.

Coaching styles

There are about as many coaching styles as there are coaches. It is not the intention here to dictate or pass any judgement on the relative benefits of one style over another. However, it is worth considering the alternatives, and the approach that is most appropriate for you. For the coach to be aware of the variety of coaching styles can only make things more interesting for all concerned.

What follows is a summary of two main approaches, but in reality the most appropriate will be your personal blend of the two. Whatever your style, bear in mind that young players all have one thing in common – they prefer to play than practice, so make sure that sessions are fun. A sense of humour on the pitch is essential as it not only keeps the coach sane, but also removes tension that can make players less inclined to extend themselves and risk making mistakes.

- **Coach in control** – this sees the coach organising and teaching in a highly structured environment. The players will be told the focus of the drill and the relevance to the game.
- **Children in control** – this model challenges the children to decide what to learn based on what is seen as important. From a controlled game environment, a development point is identified between the coach and the children. This becomes the emphasis for the session.

Traditionally the coach has been in control of the objectives of practice and has not required the children to become too involved. Clearly there must be a balance and the effective coach will blend the two and subtly guide the children. The limitations of this approach is one of overall control and available time, but it does offer the following advantages:

- Goals are set in line with confidence
- Players are engaged in more thought, and therefore learn more readily
- Children can be encouraged to develop self-coaching techniques which will be of great value to their own learning strategies.

This self-coaching principle can be introduced by skill practices being observed by one player/group that have a clear checklist of skills. This list will be the same cues that were emphasised during demonstration and coach-led introductions. This technique means that awareness of key learning points continues even when not directly participating. It also teaches observation skills that can be transferred to self-observation and to other groups.

Communication

In any sport, and on most training days, you will see a coach working with young players struggling to form groups into pre-drill formations. Instructions such as 'get into a circle' or 'I need two staggered lines' result in formations that owe more to a stage farce than a rugby session. This leads to exasperated coaches, confused children and wasted time. Never fear – here are some tips to help overcome some common problems:

Watch your language

I know an excellent tennis coach who, when working with a group of 6–8-year-olds, told them to 'stand in the tramlines'. I mentioned to him afterwards that the reason that not all of them responded was because they had no idea what a tram was, and even less of an idea about the area of court to which he was referring.

Try at all times to take account of the age and experience of players before you speak, avoid jargon like the plague, explain what you mean and constantly question and re-evaluate your use of language. If you want to test yourself, ask a non-rugby player to watch a session, and keep a list of all the terms that they do not understand. Have a look at the list and ask yourself what you really meant. For example, *drift*, *peel*, *drive*, *blind-side*, *punt* and *grubber* are just a few of the terms that you may use, but may not be easily understood by the younger players.

- **Get into pairs/groups of three**. This instruction will rarely illicit a prompt response as junior politics will come into play ('where's my best friend?'), and few want to take the initiative to move around and find a partner. For young children the best way to do this is to designate two points (or markers) as 'one' and 'two', then simply touch each player on the head, look them in the eye (important!) and give them a number. As soon as a player has a number they should go and stand at the marker. As the children get older you can pair them up by asking everyone to put their hand in the air and keep it there until they have a partner. In this way it is easier for everyone to see who remains.
- **Make a circle**. Ask a group of players (of any age) to form a circle, and what you will end up with will most likely resemble a football crowd. A good way to achieve an evenly spaced circle is simply to get all the players to hold hands and then slowly walk backwards as far as they can without letting go. If holding hands elicits too much schoolboy humour then they can grab jersey cuffs instead.
- **Form a staggered line**. In a number of the drills in this book you will need to form two parallel lines of players who are alternately spaced – a zigzag formation. This, again, can be a real struggle. The easy way to do this is in four steps:

1 Ask the players to form a single line and then hold hands/cuffs.
2 Spread them out until they can only just hold on to each other – they will then be evenly spaced.
3 Give each consecutive player a number one or two.
4 All number ones stand still. All number twos walk out to form the second line. When both lines turn to face each other you have the perfect 'zigzag'.

Group size

Consider the size of the group, and how much time each player will be waiting in line. You will need to balance appropriate rest periods with the risk of players getting cold or distracted. This will involve a bit of trial and error, but smaller is generally better as you will want to stop the drills every now and then anyway to reassert objectives and coaching points.

Quality before quantity

Building an environment of excellence can be achieved without becoming boring. Just be very clear and concise about what the skills are that you are about to practice, and then concentrate on the quality of execution at all times. Do not be drawn into lengthy drills that test stamina and reduce the quality of play – short, sharp, top-quality drills engrain top-quality play. Remember: 'Practice does not make perfect; it makes permanent.'

Session structure

There are as many ways to compile a session as there are coaches. There are some basic guidelines that will help a session make sense to players and coaches. A well-structured, controlled and brief session is much more valuable than a two-hour shambles that fizzles out because players have lost interest or are too tired.

Typical session structure

At the beginning let players know what you will be working on in the session. For young, inexperienced players it is good to pick one common skill or new technique and concentrate on that throughout – don't confuse them with trying to introduce too many things at once. (This goes for all ages at times.)

As the sessions progress and your group becomes more confident, reminders of skills covered in previous sessions are good. Remember, build on skills slowly to improve confidence, encourage quality and instil good habits.

1 Warm-up (maximum 10 minutes)

The aim is to get players ready for the session and focused on you and rugby. Include drills that introduce some basic movement techniques and dynamic stretching.

For youngsters it is important to make the warm-up fun and varied – keep it moving so they don't get bored. Don't strive for perfection – use a little imagination and they will join in with enthusiasm.

Aim to finish this section with a game-based activity from the warm-up drills to add a fun element and increase the intensity.

2 Conditioned games/controlled game scenarios (maximum 15 minutes)

Players of all ages have one thing in common – they prefer playing to practising! Make sure they get the chance to play rugby in every session, even if only for a short time.

This can be as part of a conditioned game to help introduce a skill or technique into a game situation, and as a game scenario to practise a specific move or sequence, such as a lineout or scrum. Games or conditioned games help young players learn what the game of rugby is about and help make learning permanent.

Keep players moving and changing in if you have extra numbers. Encourage observers to help watch out for good skills and give lots of praise for successes and effort. It is a good idea to set targets for players within the game other than scoring tries or kicking for goal – point scoring can be seen as the most important thing for young players and they may concentrate on this more than focusing on the team effort to gain territory and score. Set them a target for the number of tackles, interceptions of the ball, number of passes in the line, etc., whatever works for the group and you!

A sense of humour on the field is essential as it not only helps to keep the coach sane, but it will also remove tension, which can make players less inclined to try hard, leading to them making a mistake. Enjoy it and have fun!

3 Drills (maximum 25 minutes)

Select the drills depending on the objective for the session. In some cases the drills provide a natural progression and it will be clear which drills to use first. Only progress the drills if there are clear indications that the players are coping and developing good technique.

Some players will pick up the drills more easily than others; be sure to allow time to explain the drill and what you require of them and also to demonstrate the technique so they can see a good example first. Be prepared to let them try out the drill and then reset your expectations of what they need to do if necessary – remember: look for quality.

Be careful not to 'over drill' a technique – you don't want players to get bored and frustrated. There is no harm in coming back to a drill at a later stage if players are not achieving the quality you are looking for. It helps to have a couple of reserve drills up your sleeve to use at short notice if a drill is not working well – this is particularly useful when introducing some of the more complicated drills that require more concentration and coordination.

4 Warm-down and flexibility (maximum 10 minutes)

Don't skimp on this. Younger players have less need for stretching as their natural flexibility is better than in adults. However, warming down is a good habit to encourage and gives you the chance to reaffirm the skill/objective of the session and finish on a high note (i.e. 'We've just seen the value of driving on to the ball in a conditioned game and how communication makes that job much easier.').

A golden rule: always ensure lots of praise and encouragement for good effort.

NB: If you have a group of players that are involved in competitive games, you might choose to swap stages 2 and 3 around if the area for practice has already been identified. The conditioned games would then reflect the drills.

Equipment

The drills will require the following equipment:

- Cones
- Rugby balls (as many as you can lay your hands on)
- Two soccer balls (referred to in the drills as footballs)
- Bibs
- Tackle bags
- Six to eight old tyres

Improvising equipment

There are few groups that enjoy unlimited budgets, so here are some ideas for ways to improvise kit.

Ideal	Alternatives
Cones	Margarine lids and some poster paint to provide colour designations when required.
Tackle bags	Old MOD kit bags stuffed with rags are fine for smaller players. Stuffing them with scrap upholstery leather gives weight and realism to the bag. It takes a bit of searching out but is fantastic if you can get it. Make sure that buckles are removed for safety.
Bibs	Old T-shirts with the necks and arms cut off, treated with cold water dyes and spray painted letters. This might not look too grand, but is great fun for kids to make and saves lots of money.

Approach and atmosphere

The atmosphere of the training environment is vitally important, even more so with young players. An adult coach is usually a figure of authority and you must handle that responsibility with care. If you tell a player that they are useless or focus too much on a perceived failure then they will soon believe you and their confidence, along with their skill levels, will rapidly decrease. Training is a place to experiment (that's why they call it 'practice') and, as coach, part of your role is to provide an environment where the players feel free to relax, try things out, make mistakes, and in so doing, develop.

Focus on enjoyment and learning (in that order)	It's a bit obvious, but it is easier to coach a group if they come back for the next session. Focusing on building confidence in the group and individually is important; if the player believes he is improving (however low the starting point) he will likely become more interested and engaged in practice.
Be explicit and specific in the learning objective	A general statement (e.g. 'We are doing tackling practice.') is not as engaging as something specific and focused (e.g. 'We are going to work on tackles from the front. We all need to be good at this and centres, wingers and full-backs will regularly use this skill.')
Always start from an appreciative position	Focus on the development of a skill and never admonishment (e.g. 'You are all useless at catching a high ball so we are going to practice until you get it right.') A more positive approach could be, 'When we counter-attack from poor kicks we are very successful. It's important that we start with securing the kick, so we're going to spend some time working on that important first step.'

WARMING UP

The following drills provide some ideas for warming up with and without the ball, including some basic movement and mobility exercises, and some game-based activities. It doesn't matter how old players are, always follow the same rule – build speed and intensity gradually and focus on quality of movement. Start with a pulse raiser, then include some dynamic stretches, finish the warm-up with a game-based activity to keep it fun and they should be raring to go!

Working on sprinting and balance skills in warm-up drills leads to tries on the pitch – Italy's Kaine Robertson leaves France's Christophe Dominici in his wake to score in a Six Nations match.

drill 1 ball thief

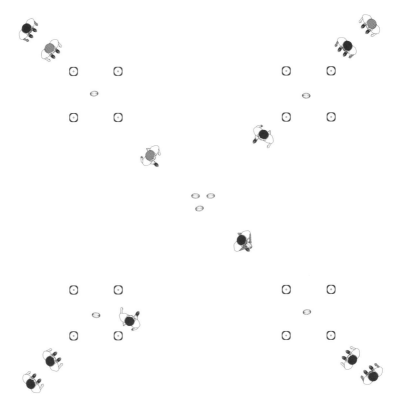

Objective: To develop communication skills and speed.

Equipment: Sixteen cones and eight balls.

Description: At each corner of a square (about 5 m wide) make a 1 m square with four cones – these will be the 'home base' for each team. Divide the players into four teams and stand them in line, one team behind each base. Place eight balls in the centre of the square. On the coach's command, one player from each team runs to the centre to grab one (and only one) ball before returning to base to place it in their square. Then the next player in line sets off to grab another ball. Once all the balls have gone from the centre the runners can steal a ball from the other bases. This continues until one team has three balls in their home base. If no one wins within a set time the coach can add another ball to make success a little easier.

Coaching points: Watch for cheats picking up two balls at a time. Encourage each team to talk to their runner to make him aware of what else is going on.

drill 2   horse and jockey

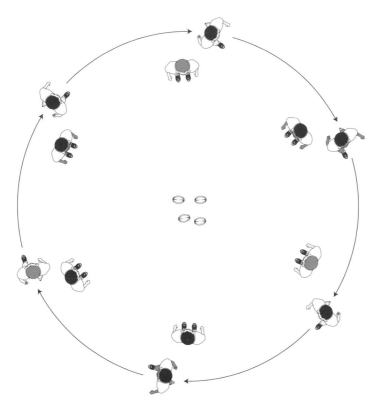

Objective: To warm up the body.

Equipment: Several balls.

Description: Arrange the players into two circles, one inside the other. A number of balls are placed in the middle of the inner circle. On the call of 'left' or 'right' the players in the outside circle have to run in that direction around the entire circle. Once the players get back to their starting position they must go through the legs of a player in the inner circle, grab a ball and return to their start position. Players need to be on their feet before going for a ball. The idea is that there are fewer balls than there are players to grab them.

Coaching points: Ensure plenty of rest between goes. This will ensure that the players practise high-quality speed and agility over a short distance.

drill 3 zigzag shuttles

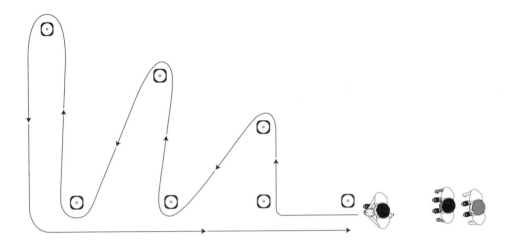

Objective: To warm up by practising sprinting and changing direction.

Equipment: Seven cones and four balls.

Description: Set out the cones as shown above, with the first cone positioned on the corner of the try line and touchline. Players line up off up the touchline from behind this cone. On the coach's command, the first player jogs up to the second cone, turns sharply and sprints to the third cone, turns and jogs up to the fourth cone and so on through the grid as shown, before rejoining the back of the line and waiting his turn to go again. Every player should run holding a ball with both hands in front of the body.

Coaching points: Focus on the need to step sharply off the outside foot to change direction – keep the distances between cones short (maximum five strides). When driving for acceleration, encourage the players to take smaller steps for the first two or three strides to push off hard, lean slightly forwards, use their arms to help propel themselves forwards and look where they are going, not at the floor. It may help for them to exaggerate a high knee lift – this can help stop feet dragging especially when players are not used to controlling this movement, or are going through growth spurts and coping with gangly limbs! Let the first runner get through two cones before the next runner sets off. Keep the groups large enough that each runner has a good long recovery, but small enough that they do not get cold.

Progression: Ask the runner to start with the ball in two hands and shift it to one hand at each change of direction. The ball should always be on the inside arm (as if the runner is fending off a would-be tackler coming in from the outside). Return the ball to two hands during the jog phases.

drill 4   snakes

Objective: To warm up and have fun.

Equipment: One football per team.

Description: Divide the group into teams with a maximum of six players per team. Each team lines up one behind the other, 1 m apart with legs apart. Player A is the last player in the line and has the ball. On the coach's command, A rolls the ball through the legs of the players in the line, then races to take up position at the head of the line and catch his own roll. Once in possession of the ball and still facing forwards, he picks up the ball and twists his trunk to pass the ball to the player behind, who takes the ball two handed and twists the opposite way to the next player. This left/right twisting motion is repeated until the ball is back with the player at the back of the line, who starts the drill again by rolling the ball through the tunnel of legs once more. Repeat until all players have rolled.

Coaching points: While this is a 'young' drill, the twisting motion is a great warm-up for the upper body, and with the two teams racing each other it can be a lot of fun.

drill 5 dodge tag

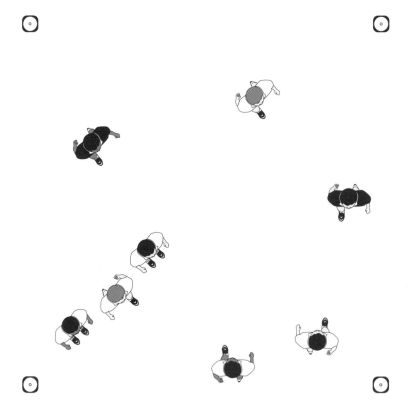

Objective: To practise dodging skills and improve balanced movement.

Equipment: Players.

Description: The playing area selected should be sufficient to allow the number of players to run around but not so large that it allows full freedom of movement. Ideally you should aim to have eight players in a 10 m square area. Use cones to mark the area. Two players are taggers (in black above). The rest of the players must dodge out of their way and avoid being tagged. Players who have been tagged must stand still, creating barriers for the other players to dodge around.

Coaching points: Encourage players to make a definite dodge move to avoid the obstacles. Look for quick changes of direction, pushing off the outside foot and using hips and shoulders to help keep balanced. All footwork should be balanced and controlled.

Progression: Reduce the size of the playing area and increase the number of taggers.

drill 6 reverse wrestling

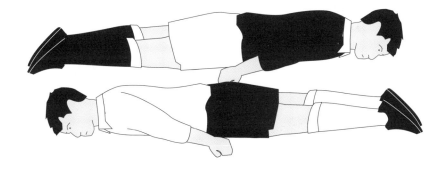

Objective: A controlled contact warm-up.

Equipment: Players.

Description: Assign players into pairs, and lie face down top-to-toe. On the coach's command, it's a straight race to see who can stand up first. Encourage players to stop their opponent in any way that is permitted within the rules of rugby (strictly no punching, kicking or gouging).

Coaching points: Try, wherever possible, to match up players by size.

drill 7 dynamic stretches

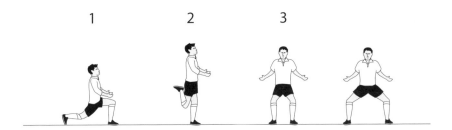

| 1 | 2 | 3 |

Objective: To stretch main muscle groups as part of the warm-up.

Equipment: Players.

Description: Line up the players along the sideline. Working together, they move across the pitch performing the following movements:

- **lunge** – alternate legs. A wide stride forwards and a deep lunge bending both legs to right angles.
- **heel flicks** – heels kick up to the bottom. Look for as many quick heel flicks as possible across the area.
- **sumo squats** – facing towards one post, the body remains upright and taking a wide stance the player squats down low and then returns to standing. Repeat 5 times then turn and face the other post and repeat.

Work across the pitch in equal working areas for each dynamic stretch. Repeat back across pitch to starting point.

Coaching points: Focus on controlled movements and balance – speed is not important. With the lunge, remind players that the front knee should stay behind the toes and they need to keep an upright body.

drill 8   work that ball

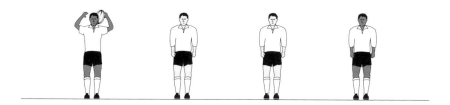

Objective: To warm up with the ball and help develop confidence controlling the movement of the ball.

Equipment: One ball to every group of players – group in fours, fives or sixes.

Description: Start the groups standing in lines approximately 3 m apart and close enough to each other to be able to reach the ball from the person next to them – as shown in the diagram. The first player in each line has the ball. This drill can be performed as a relay race or in single groups. On the coach's command the first player passes the ball twice round their head and twice round their middle and then gives the ball to the next player who does the same. The ball passes down the line and when the last player has completed the ball rotations they run round the back of the line to take up position at the starting point and the drill begins again. Repeat this until the starting player is back at the front of the line with the ball.

Coaching points: Focus on controlled, quick movements of the ball. Younger players tend to rush, especially if they're in a race situation, and they can lose concentration and then control of the ball. The number of rotations around the body can be increased.

drill 9   passing warm-up

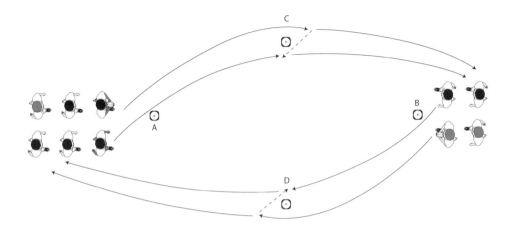

Objective: To warm up with the ball and help develop confidence in passing.

Equipment: Two groups of players working in pairs with one ball.

Description: Set up the working area as shown with one group starting behind cones A and B. The first pair from each group jogs out in an arc towards cones C and D – as shown. The ball carrier jogs around the outside of the cone in a wider arc than their team-mate who jogs on the inside of the cone behind the ball carrier. The ball carrier passes the ball to the receiver at the cone. Both players continue jogging and join the line behind the opposite cone to their start point. The drill continues.

Coaching points: Start slowly and build up speed as confidence and accuracy in passing improves. Focus on controlled passing of the ball with the receiver having hands ready as a target for the passer and to catch the ball. The receiver needs to time his run to the inside of the cone so he is behind the ball carrier at the time of the pass.

drill 10 ball tag

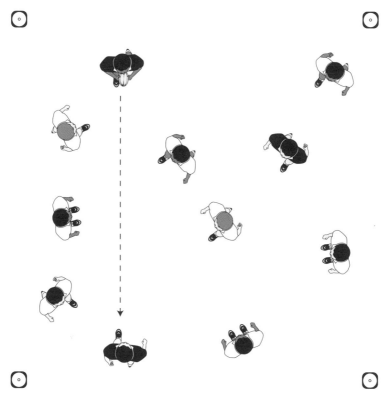

Objective: To develop communication skills, speed and awareness of other players.

Equipment: Four cones and one ball.

Description: Create a square using the cones (about 5–10 m wide). Three attackers and numerous evaders work within each square, and the objective is for the attackers to tag the evaders with the ball. Once tagged the evader must stand still. The attackers can pass the ball to each other, but once they are in possession they can only pivot on one foot. 'Free' evaders must be aware of stationary 'tagged' evaders, and move and dodge around them.

Coaching points: Encourage lots of communication and movement between attackers, and look for quick but accurate passing.

Progression: Change the attackers regularly and see how many victims they tag in a fixed time (say two minutes).

SPEED DEVELOPMENT

Good rugby players are able to demonstrate quick changes of pace and good sprinting technique, enabling them to drive into space and evade defenders in attacking play to gain territory and score tries. These skills require balance, strength and control of body movement – something that younger players need to develop and practise.

This chapter lists drills to help develop strength and balance and to practise change of pace and sprinting techniques.

Demonstrating good high knee lift and use of the arms, George North, the Wales winger, training in preparation for the autumn internationals.

drill 11 fast feet

Objective: To develop foot speed, balance and control of movement.

Equipment: Players.

Description: The players stand on the sideline facing in-field to the 5 m line. Using very fast feet and tiny steps, the players move towards the 5 m line. When the players reach the 5 m line they turn and walk slowly back to the sideline and start again. The objective is to complete as many tiny steps in the shortest amount of time possible.

Coaching points: Younger children will lose concentration and form very quickly and will increase the length of their steps in order to move forwards more quickly. Re-emphasise the 'fast feet and tiny steps' before each start. Encourage players to use their arms in a pumping action to help with balance. They may also need to lift their knees to avoid dragging their feet – you do not want to ask for high knees as in previous drills as the aim is to make quick contact with the floor. Get them to experiment to get the feel of moving their 'fast feet' as fast as possible. The race is not to see who moves forwards fastest, but rather who can get the most steps in over the specified distance.

Progression: Try a timed race – who can perform the most steps in 10 seconds?

drill 12 side jumps

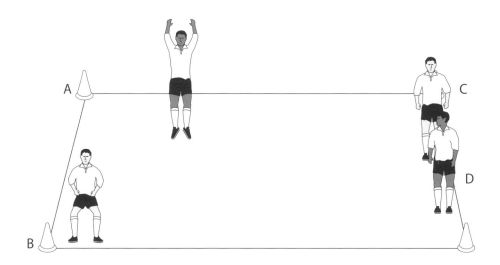

Objective: To improve general agility; to condition the groin muscles (adductors and abductors); to prevent imbalance injuries and stabilise the prime muscle groups.

Equipment: Players.

Description: Split the group into four lines (A, B, C and D), with A and B on one sideline and C and D on the other. All players face up the grid so they are side on to each other. With good posture, line A side-jumps across aiming for height and distance on each jump. Line C then begins the drill, and so on.

Coaching points: Insist on quality at all times. Allow lots of recovery between sets. As players tire there will be a tendency for bodies to sag and for players to twist into a run. Looking backwards to where they came from will help players keep their bodies in the correct position. There is no need for fast forward movements – height and 'hang time' are what you want to see.

Progression: With older players encourage criticism and observation so they become their own coaches. Remind them that form and quality are everything.

drill 13 high kicks

Objective: To develop strength and movement skills.

Equipment: Players.

Description: Starting on the sideline, players march out to the centre of the court performing a series of high kicks, clapping their hands under the thigh with each stride. Each leg lift must be as high as possible and the drill must be performed under control. The objective is perfect form, not speed.

Coaching points: Insist on straight legs during this movement. Don't allow the body to curl towards the knee. It doesn't matter how high the straight leg comes as long as the form is perfect. Over a period of time the range of movement will improve and develop.

drill 14 high knees

Objective: To condition the hip flexors; to learn to lift knees fast and high when running to aid stride length, reduce foot-to-ground contact time and therefore increase speed.

Equipment: Players.

Description: Split the group into four lines (A, B, C and D). A and B stand on one sideline with lines C and D facing them on the other sideline. Line A runs slowly forwards with knees pulled fast and high to the chest, keeping the thighs in line with the direction of running. When they reach the other side, line C begins the drill, then line B and so on. In this way each line has plenty of recovery time.

Coaching points: Insist on quality at all times. Allow lots of recovery time in between sets. As players tire there will be a tendency for bodies to sag and knees to splay outwards. If this happens, stop the players and re-assert the aim to bring the knees up to the chest, not the other way around. There is no need for fast forward motion – foot speed and a high knee lift are everything here. Encourage players to keep their body upright, eyes looking where they are going and to use their arms in a pumping action to help with balance. Three runs for each group is plenty – mix it in with the other speed drills as part of a post-warm-up.

Progression: With older players, encourage criticism and observation so they become their own coaches. Remember that form and quality are everything.

high skipping

Objective: To condition the hip flexors, extensors and calf muscles; to teach forceful and short ground contact time in order to develop speed.

Equipment: Players.

Description: Split the group into four lines (A, B, C and D), A and B on one sideline and C and D on the other. With good posture, line A high-skips across the area. When they reach the other line, line C begins the drill and so on.

Coaching points: Insist on quality at all times. Allow lots of recovery between sets. Teach good, tall posture with the top of the head held high. The players should aim for greatest possible height and knee lift, with the front leg raised so that the soles of the shoes are visible to observers in front. Use the arms to assist lift.

Progression: With older players, encourage criticism and observation so they become their own coaches. Remind them that form and quality are everything.

drill 16 back to backs

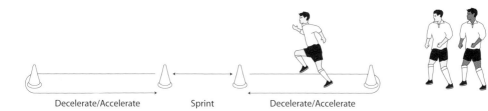

Decelerate/Accelerate   Sprint   Decelerate/Accelerate

Objective: To develop speed and endurance.

Equipment: Four cones.

Description: Mark out a run of 10 m, then 5 m, then 10 m. Players gently accelerate from the first to the second cone, then run flat out for 5 m. They then use the final 10 m to decelerate, turn straight around and start accelerating to the second cone to perform the drill again. There and back is one rep. Each player completes two reps and then walks slowly to fully recover before going again. Start with three sets of two reps and build up slowly over a period of weeks.

Coaching points: Encourage a real change of pace and controlled movement. At the point of acceleration ask players to take smaller steps for the first two or three strides to push off hard, lean slightly forwards, use their arms to help propel themselves forwards and look where they are going. Stride length increases as they gain speed. Encourage players to use a high knee lift (not an exaggerated lift as in the previous drill), just enough to help avoid feet dragging on the floor. They should 'pump' their arms to help with balance.

Progression: Use stopwatches to record times over the middle 5 m. Increase reps by one or two per session while ensuring the quality of the middle section is maintained.

drill 17 hollow sprints

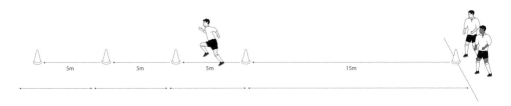

Objective: To develop a marked change of pace.

Equipment: Four cones.

Description: Place the cones in a line – the first cone to be placed at 15 m from the touchline, and the remaining three at 5 m intervals. Starting at the touch-line, players gently accelerate over the first 15 m to reach full pace at the first marker, hold full pace until the second marker, decelerate to three-quarter pace until the third marker and sharply accelerate to full pace until the last cone. Walk back to the start slowly to recover.

Coaching points: Here the players are training their bodies to go fast, so they need to perform this drill while they are reasonably fresh. You must also allow plenty of rest between sets to ensure that every set is top quality. If you use this drill when players are tired they will never get the feeling of travelling fast. Tell the players to concentrate on how it feels. When they accelerate players should take smaller steps for the first two or three strides to push off hard, lean slightly forwards, use their arms to help propel themselves forwards and look where they are going. Stride length increases. Look for balanced, definite changes of speed at the marker point to develop control of pace.

BALL HANDLING AND ATTACKING

Attacking space and continuous play with the ball being passed quickly from set-piece play and second or subsequent phases of play are essential for success on the rugby field. Having control of the ball and creating options for players to gain territory helps teams to score points.

Ball handling is an obvious key element of rugby. Young players need to develop confidence in their catching and throwing, how the ball feels, react to different situations and retain control of the ball even with defensive pressure.

It is important to provide opportunities to practise ball handling in game situations as well as in drills. This encourages players to develop their decision-making skills and tactical awareness, such as being able to offload in contact situations, knowing when to make the pass and when to hold on to the ball, who to pass to, getting the timing of the pass etc. The ability to make these decisions and read the game is as important as having the technical skill for a good rugby player.

Another key attacking skill is the side-step – the ability to step quickly around a tackler at pace and keep moving towards the goal line. This is particularly useful for avoiding a tackle and creating more options to gain territory and score.

To side-step well a player needs fast feet and the ability to think quickly. Encouraging a young player to quickly decide when and on which side to make a quick side-step in a game situation, followed by a straight-line sprint towards the goal line, can take time as they develop confidence. Don't give up, and focus on the basics, building up the complexity slowly as ability and experience develop.

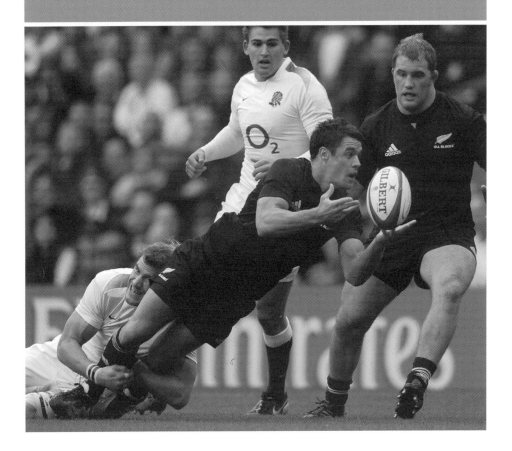

The All Black Dan Carter makes a crucial pass to continue New Zealand's attack, despite being tackled by England's Tom Croft.

drill 18 catch-up squares

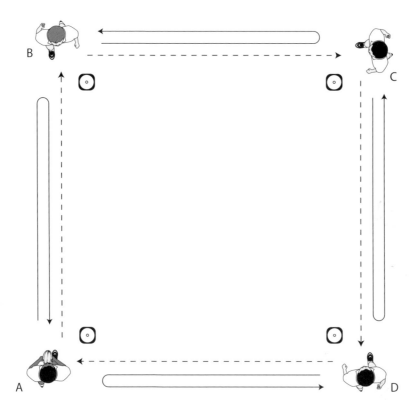

Objective: To improve passing and movement skills.

Equipment: Four cones and one ball.

Description: Set up a square with the cones about 3 m apart. Player A starts with the ball, and passes to player B. Having given the pass, player A follows it by running to player B and then returning to their starting point. Play continues in this way around the grid.

Coaching points: The key coaching point is to ensure that everyone concentrates on giving a good pass and not just 'unloading' the ball in panic. Remind players that the ball will always travel faster than they do – a valuable lesson in itself!

Progression: When the principle of the drill is mastered, start with an extra ball at the opposite corner. The objective is for one of the balls to catch up with the other, or to play for one minute – whichever comes first.

drill 19 passing 1

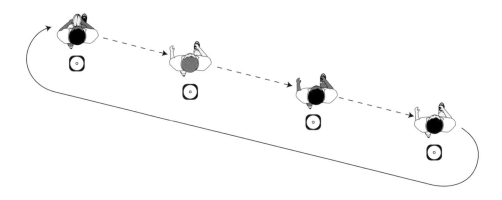

Objective: To introduce basic passing and catching skills.

Equipment: Four cones and one ball.

Description: Place the cones in a gently staggered line, approximately 1.5 m apart. On the coach's command the ball is passed down the line from player to player. When the last player has the ball, he runs around to the first cone, and the rest of the line moves one cone to the right. Play continues until all players have passed at each position. To change the direction of passing, stop the drill and have the players face the opposite direction, so the stagger will be reversed.

Coaching points: The pass should be a smooth movement across the body with a focus on the hands, wrists and arms making the pass, rather than the shoulders. Encourage the ball carrier to look for the receiver's hands as a target to pass to. When the ball is coming from the left players should stand with their right foot slightly forward, shoulders rotated towards the passer and their hands up ready to receive the ball. Change feet when the ball is coming from the other direction.

Progression: Ask the players to run on the spot while completing the same drill.

drill 20 passing 2

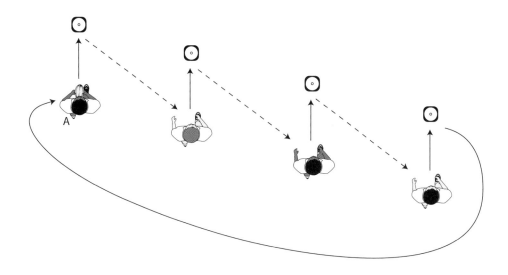

Objective: To introduce passing and catching skills on the move.

Equipment: Four cones and one ball.

Description: Place the cones in a gently staggered line, approximately 1.5 m apart, with each player standing 1 m behind their cone. On the coach's command player A walks up to his cone and when he reaches it, he passes the ball to the second player, who in turn has walked up to their cone to collect the pass. When the last player has the ball, he runs around to the first cone, and the rest of the line moves one cone to the right. Play continues until all players have passed at each position. To change the direction of passing, stop the drill and have the players face the opposite direction, so the stagger will be reversed.

Coaching points: This simple drill will be a challenge for some younger players as they have to move, think and execute a skill all at once. It is very important they have a clear, concise understanding of the passing and catching skill set – body turned towards the ball and hands up to receive, focus on a spot on the ball to catch and a smooth movement across the body to the receiver. This drill introduces the concept of timing a walk. Make sure that the walk is at a steady pace so that the catch and pass is completed with a single stride. When the players are resting, talk with them about how they could improve their timing.

drill 21 passing 3

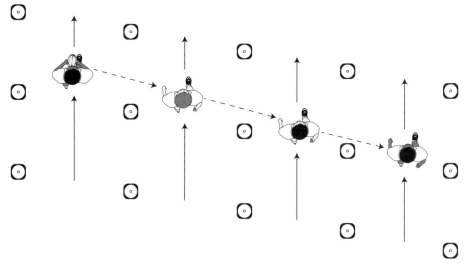

Objective: To develop passing and catching skills on the move.

Equipment: Fifteen cones and one ball.

Description: Place the cones in a gently staggered line as before. 10 m ahead make another staggered line, with a final line in the centre of the grid. This creates four 'channels' for players to run in. On the coach's command, the first player jogs out and just after the second cone passes to the second player, who in turn has jogged out but remained a few paces behind. The second player then runs for two or three strides before passing to the third player. When the last player has the ball, he runs around to the first cone, and the rest of the line moves one cone to the right. Play continues until all players have passed at each position. To change the direction of passing, stop the drill and have the players face the opposite direction, so the stagger will be reversed.

Coaching points: The catcher must keep a slight distance behind the passer, and be encouraged to run on to the ball. The watchwords are 'run when you have the ball, hold back when you are waiting to receive and then run on to the ball'. Once a player has passed he must slow down to allow the ball carrier to overtake him. This important concept is at the core of playing rugby – staying behind the ball at all times. As in the previous drills it is very important to continue to reiterate a clear, concise understanding of the passing and catching skill set. Remind the players what they told you about when they should run, what a well set line looks like, etc.

Progression: Increase the speed of running. Once players have mastered the drill you can introduce timed races between groups with penalties for a dropped ball, running out of their channel or a player getting in front of the ball.

drill 22 passing 4

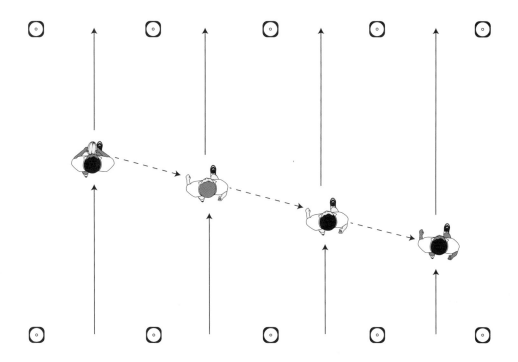

Objective: To improve passing and catching skills on the move.

Equipment: Ten cones and one ball.

Description: Place five cones in a straight line, approximately 2 m apart with another line 15 m opposite. The first player has the ball and on the coach's command he jogs out and passes along the line. When the line reaches the other side of the grid they pause to realign and then return.

Coaching points: The progression from the previous drill is that players do not have a ready-made stagger in the passing line so they must time their run to allow the player with the ball to move ahead.

Progression: Ask players to increase their speed of running. Add a second line to run from the opposite side of the grid at the same time.

drill 23 jump and catch

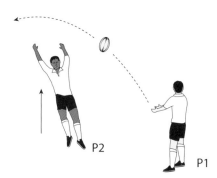

P2

P1

P2

P1

Objective: To develop confidence and practise catching a high ball.

Equipment: Players in pairs with one ball.

Description: Players stand facing each other approximately 3 m apart. Player 1 starts with the ball and throws a high ball in front of player 2 who jumps to catch the ball, aiming to catch it at the highest point. He lands and throws a high ball for player 1. Repeat for a set number of throws. This drill can be performed in groups or as a relay race.

Coaching points: Focus on the receiver timing his jump so he can catch the ball at the highest point rather than waiting for the ball to fall to him. Encourage him to lead the jump with a high left or right knee and use his arms to help get height. Players should land with a wide stance to help with balance.

Progression: The jumping player turns in the air when catching the ball to land facing the opposite way – as if to shield the ball from a defender. When players can consistently catch and turn, progress to a high over-the-shoulder pass where the receiver has to turn and track under the ball before timing his jump to catch.

moving with the ball

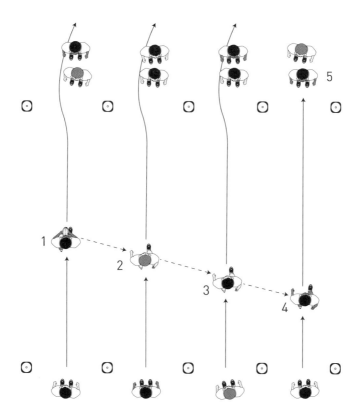

Objective: To introduce handling skills on the move.

Equipment: Ten cones and one ball.

Description: Set up a 10 m square grid with two lines of 5 cones placed 2 m apart. Two players are assigned to stand behind each cone, and the ball is with player 1. On the coach's command, player 1 runs out and passes to player 2, and so forth along the line. When player 4 receives the ball, he continues his run and passes to player 5 who brings his lineout and passes as before. The drill continues until all four groups have run.

Coaching points: Players should have their hands up to receive the ball. The ball should move smoothly across the front of the body as they pass, and they must look for the receiver's hands as a target to pass to.

drill 25 find the space

Start

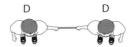

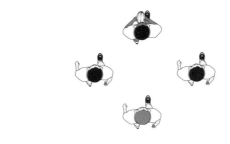

Objective: To develop confidence in passing on the move, communication and decision-making skills.

Equipment: Groups of six, one ball, one tag belt or band, four cones.

Description: Set up a grid area 10 m x 10 m (the size can vary depending on the ability of the group). Two defenders hold a band or belt between them to act as a barrier. The other four in the group are attackers and have the ball. Starting on one side of the square in a diamond shape – as shown – the attackers must pass the ball between each other aiming to reach the other sideline and score a try. They must form an attacking line to allow the pass to be behind – see diagram 2. The defenders must work together to try to create a barrier for the attackers and stop them moving into the space. The attackers must react to the defenders and try to find different space for their passing to progress across the area.

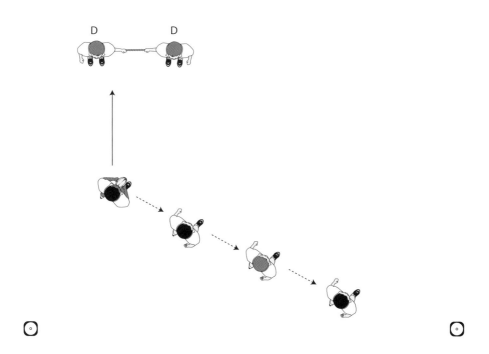

Coaching points: This involves players thinking and reacting to each other so start slowly with more inexperienced or younger players. Let them get the feel of moving into the space and changing the direction of the passing to avoid the defenders. Look for formation of the attacking line after a start from the diamond shape and encourage lots of communication between attackers. Defenders also need to communicate and work together – there shouldn't be any contact between the attackers and defenders. Increase the pace of the attackers when they are more confident and look for them driving into the space to cross the area.

Progression: Increase the working area, number of defending pairs and attackers. Take care for the drill not to lose form.

drill 26 fast hands

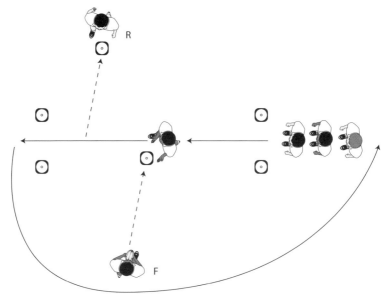

Objective: To develop the ability to give and take a pass quickly.

Equipment: Five cones and one ball.

Description: Place the cones as shown in the diagram. The distance between players F and R depends on their experience. Start with 3 m – it can always be increased. The first player jogs out from the starting position. Upon reaching the central cone he is fed a pass by player F and passes it on to player R. He finishes by running between the final two cones, and then rejoins the back of the line ready to repeat. Keep rotating the players and keep groups small so that there is not too much waiting time. Change the direction of running to practise passing off the other hand.

Coaching points: There will be a tendency for players to drift away from the ball carrier and run at an angle away from the pass. In a game this would reduce the amount of space available for the attacking team as they move towards the sideline. To avoid this, encourage players to run straight. Make sure they run with their hands up ready to receive the pass with their palms facing the passer, and look at the ball as they catch it. The ball should move smoothly across the front of the body as they pass, and they must look for the receiver's hands as a target to pass to.

Progression: Increase the running speed and then reduce the distance between F and R to reduce the time in which to make the pass. As confidence grows, ask player R to alternate between open hands and closed fists. The runner can only pass to open hands, and so must look at the receiver. If the runner sees fists he holds the ball and runs hard through the final two cones.

drill 27   fast hands under pressure

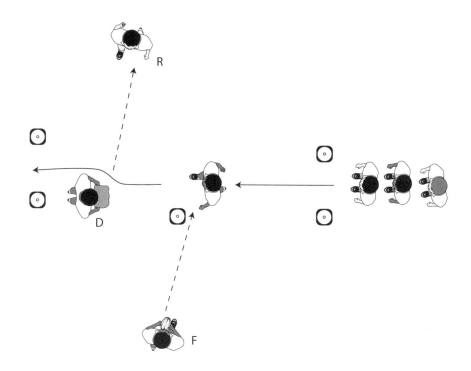

Objective: To improve the ability to give and take a pass quickly.

Equipment: Five cones, one ball and one tackle shield.

Description: Set up the cones as in the previous drill. As before, the first player jogs out from the starting position. Upon reaching the central cone he is fed a pass by player F and passes it on to player R. He finishes by running between the final two cones, and then rejoins the back of the line ready to repeat. The progression in this drill comes from the addition of a player with a tackle shield (player D) who steps up to pressurise the pass. Change the direction of running to practise passing off the other hand.

Coaching points: There will be an even greater tendency for players to drift away from the pass as the pressure comes on from the shield, so remind players to run straight. The runner should continue to focus on the ball and the receiver at all times but should get a feel for checking slightly as the pass is made.

Progression: Initially the shield is only there as a passive obstacle. As skills develop, the player with the shield can take a step towards the runner to increase the pressure.

drill 28 pick and flick

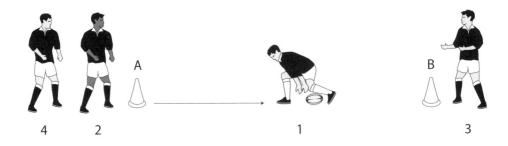

A

B

4   2   1   3

Objective: To develop a flicked pass from the floor while on the move.

Equipment: Two cones and one ball per team.

Description: Divide the players into teams of no more than four. The two cones (A and B) are set 5 m apart. The ball is placed 2 m in front of cone A. Player 1 runs out and passes the ball from the floor to player 2 who is standing behind cone A, before running through to join the back of the line opposite. Player 2 now places the ball 2 m in front of cone B and runs through to join the back of the line opposite. Player 3 now runs out and passes the ball from the floor to player 4, and so the drill continues.

Coaching points: When introducing the drill, allow the players to move towards the ball at a brisk walk – positioning of the feet is vital and correct technique must be emphasised above speed. When picking the ball up, the rear foot should be beside the ball and the front foot towards the target receiver. The movement is to 'sweep' the ball from the floor rather than to pick it up and then pass. Players should bend the knees rather than the back, as this will allow them to keep their head up and spot the target. Receivers always provide a target with hands up ready.

Progression: Increase the distances slightly.

drill 29 pick and pass

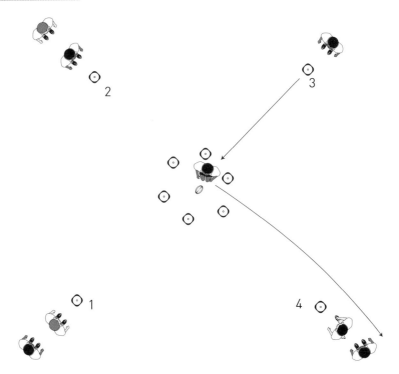

Objective: To develop a pass from the floor while on the move.

Equipment: Ten cones and one ball.

Description: Place six cones in a 1 m diameter circle. Place another four cones 3 m away, as shown in the diagram, with a maximum of three players assigned to each of these cones. Each outer cone is numbered 1–4, and the ball is placed in the centre circle. When the coach calls a number and a direction (e.g. 'one-left'), the first player from the designated cone runs out and passes the ball from the floor in the direction indicated, before running through to join the back of the line directly opposite. The receiver then runs out and places the ball in the circle, before running through and joining the rear of the line opposite. The coach then calls out another number and direction, and so the drill continues.

Coaching points: As before, when picking the ball up the rear foot should be beside the ball and towards the target receiver. The movement is to 'sweep' the ball from the floor rather than to pick it up and then pass. Players should bend the knees rather than the back, as this will allow them to keep their head up and spot the target. Receivers always provide a target with hands up ready. The coach must make it clear that as players move around the grid their number will change accordingly.

attacking from broken play

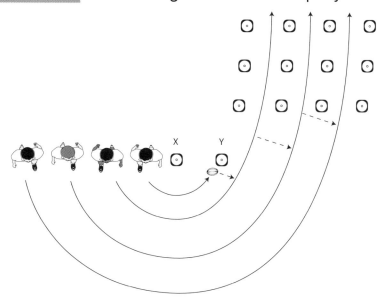

Objective: To structure an attacking line from a broken play situation.

Equipment: Twelve cones and one ball for every four players.

Description: Place the cones in lines, with each cone 1 m apart and each line of cones 2 m from the next, as shown in the diagram. Players start as a group at cone X with a ball at cone Y. Each player is given a number 1–4. To start the drill the coach calls a number. The player called becomes the scrum-half and runs to the ball ready to feed the first player. At the same time all the other players run around cone Y and turn to attack up the grid. The drill is complete when the ball reaches the far end of the grid.

Coaching points: This drill requires the players to time their run to ensure that they are in a position to run onto the ball. The cones create channels for each player to run in. The players must run the corner hard so they are facing up the grid and not across it. There is a tendency for players to drift away from the ball and across the grid. A drift is usually a sign that the players are either:

- not timing their run and are forced to move sideways to avoid over-running the pass or;
- not running the corner hard enough and therefore entering the grid running laterally.

Progression: Ask the players to start by walking in a tight circle around cone X. On the coach's command they must start to run. As there is no designated scrum-half, a player must call for the ball and all other players must communicate with each other to say who has which channel.

drill 31 combination skills

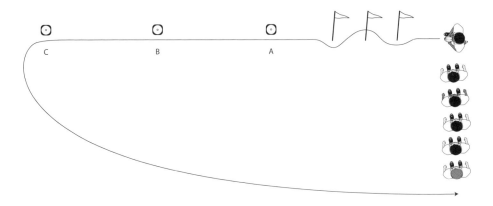

Objective: To introduce a variety of handling skills in a competitive environment.

Equipment: Three cones 10 m apart, three flags 2 m apart and a ball per team.

Description: Split the players into teams of five, and set out the drill area for each team as shown. On the coach's command, each team sets off with the first player carrying the ball, running in and out of the flags. When the ball carrier reaches cone A he places the ball firmly on the floor (as if scoring a try) and runs on to cone B to form the opposition. The second player in line scoops up the try, and makes contact with the opposition on cone B. He hits and falls using the count of three (one = hit, two = down, three = lay back the ball.) The third player then picks up the lay back ball and races to cone C where he simulates a tackle and goes down, protecting the ball. Rolling onto his back he delivers a pop pass to the fourth player who runs past and gives a pass to the fifth player. They then return to the start.

Coaching points: Identify with the players the skills involved; protecting the ball, looking at the ball, using both hands where possible. Timing is vital – if supporting players are too early the line stutters and loses its speed, so they must learn to be slightly late if anything. This will add to the speed of the ball and create a smooth flow of play.

Progression: Hold competitions – which team can do three circuits without a mistake? Which team is the fastest over one, two or three circuits. Pressure is important.

side-step 1

Objective: To introduce side-stepping skills.

Equipment: Four cones and two balls per team.

Description: Divide the players into teams of six. Place the cones as shown, with the two centre cones 1 m apart. Half the team lines up behind cone A, and the other half lines up behind cone D. On the coach's command, the first players from each team run with the ball towards each other. When they reach the centre cones the players step sharply to their right and then straighten up to run through to the next player in line. Change to a step to the left when all players have had a turn.

Coaching points: Make sure that both players run straight, and that there is a definite quick change of direction by pushing off hard on the appropriate leg. Encourage players to use their eyes and their head to 'sell' their intention to go one way before planting and driving off the outside foot to step the other way. This is the basis of a successful side-step as much as anything else. Look for controlled, balanced movement with body upright.

Progression: As confidence grows, decrease the space between the centre cones and increase speed.

drill 33 side step 2

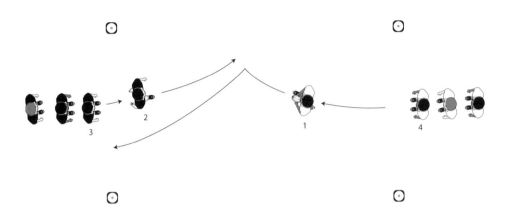

Objective: To develop side-stepping skills.

Equipment: Four cones and one ball per team.

Description: Place the cones as shown, forming a rectangle 5 m x 10 m. Split the players into teams of four. Two teams line up opposite each other at either end of the grid. On the coach's command, player 1 jogs out with the ball in an arc to the right to draw player 2 across the grid. Just before player 1 reaches player 2, he steps sharply to the left and then on to the end of the grid where he passes to player 3 who becomes the attacker, and so the drill continues.

Coaching points: Players can use this drill to experiment how far they need to draw the defender in and across before they step. They can also try to use their shoulder to help 'sell' their intention to step one way – a slight dip in the shoulder to the left with eyes and head moving to the left before a quick side-step to the right. This needs practise to perfect the timing and convince the defender. This drill can also form the start of the defensive skill by showing how the defender can guard against a side-step by staying on the inside shoulder and forcing the ball carrier towards the edge of the grid – the touchline.

Progression: As skills develop, players should gradually increase speed.

drill 34   fixing a defender – two on one

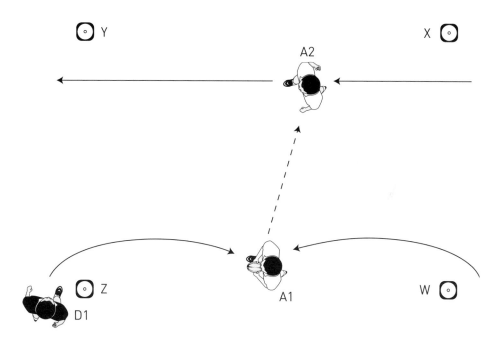

Objective: To teach players how to hold a defender to make space for an attacking team-mate; to time a pass.

Equipment: Four cones and one ball for every team.

Description: Divide the players into teams of four. Place the cones as shown, creating a 5 m by 10 m grid. The attacking player A1 has the ball on cone W and the defending player D1 is on cone Z. Player A2 stands between cones X and Y. On the coach's command, the players enter the grid. The objective for A1 is to make the defender stand still (to 'fix' them) and time a pass to A2 for him to score at the far end of the grid. The defender aims to tag tackle or block the pass.

Coaching points: This is a progression from the previous drill so it is important to carry over the learning. The attacker must run straight at (or slightly to the inside shoulder of) the defender. Any drift will allow the defender to track across and run the attacker out of space against the far boundary of the grid. A2 must time his run relative to A1 to ensure that he takes the ball at close to full speed, travelling straight. After a few runs the defenders may get wise, and now the attacker must run out slightly to create space on both sides of the defender before straightening up and 'fixing'.

Progression: Introduce some competition – 3 points for a score by A2, 1 point for a score by A1, 5 points deducted for a successful defence.

drill 35 passing out of a tackle

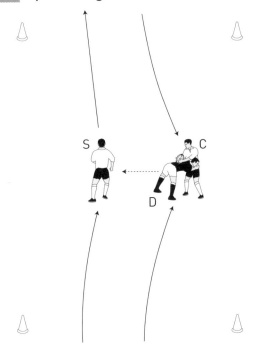

Objective: To introduce the skills required to pass out of a tackle to a supporting player.

Equipment: Four cones, one ball per team and target stickers.

Description: Divide the players into teams of three (ball carrier = C; support runner = S; defender = D) and place target stickers on the thighs of each player. Place the cones as shown, creating a 5 m × 10 m grid. Groups line up one behind the other – players C and S at one end, and D at the other. On the coach's command, player C walks briskly down the centre of the grid with the ball, and player D moves to meet him. As he approaches player D he arcs out slightly to the left to ensure that the tackle is more from the side. As D comes in to tackle, C reaches through the tackle and pops a pass up to S who is running just to the left of the defender. Repeat the drill with all players rotating starting positions, and ensuring that passes to the left and right are completed.

Coaching points: It is important that the ball carriers get the feeling of moving the defender with the angle of their run so that they can free up enough space to pass through the tackle. The supporting runner must run close to the tackle and must time the run correctly.

Progression: As skills develop, players should gradually increase speed.

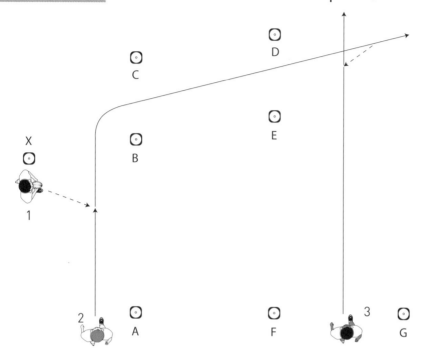

Objective: To develop the scissor move (reverse pass) and practise drawing defenders out of position.

Equipment: Eight cones and one ball per team.

Description: Divide the players into teams of three. Place the cones as shown in the diagram. Player 1 has the ball at cone X, player 2 stands to the left of cone A and player 3 stands to the right of cone F. On the coach's command, player 2 runs out to receive a pass from player 1, and then runs on to cone B where he cuts across field using the channel made by cones B–C and D–E. Player 3 runs straight ahead to take the scissor pass on the inside of player 2.

Coaching points: The channel is put in place to force the ball carrier to execute a definite change of direction, and prevent them from running a 'lazy' arc. The principle of this move is to draw defenders out of position – player 2 must first 'interest' the defender by running forwards and then changing direction, causing the defender to come with him. The reverse, or scissor pass, sends player 3 into the resulting gap. Timing is everything – this drill allows players to experiment with how late they can leave a run and what happens if they crowd the pass.

Progression: Remove the cones, and see if the lines of running alter. The most common effect is that players immediately drift rather than running up and then across in a definite change of direction.

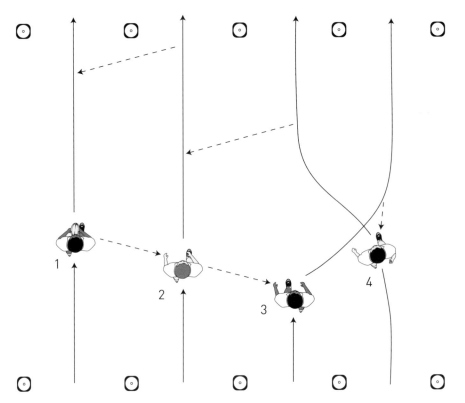

Objective: To develop the scissor move (reverse pass).

Equipment: Ten cones and one ball per team.

Description: Set up cones into eight gates as shown. On the coach's command, player 1 runs out and the ball is passed to player 2 and player 3 in turn. Player 3 now cuts across field and player 4 runs to take the scissor pass on the inside of player 3. Player 4 then passes the ball back to player 2, who in turn passes it back to player 1. The team finishes by running through the gates at the far side of the grid. Change positions and repeat the drill.

Coaching points: Watch the timing of player 4, as there will be a tendency to anticipate the move and the player may have to slow down to take the pass.

Progression: Once the players have mastered this skill, ask them to complete a scissor on the return pass – player 4 passes to player 2 who cuts across player 1 and takes the scissor pass.

drill 38   run-around or loop

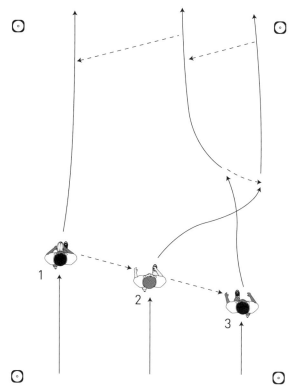

Objective: To introduce the run-around or loop pass.

Equipment: Four cones and one ball per team.

Description: Place the cones as shown, creating a 5 m × 8 m grid. Divide the players into teams of three, and ask them to line up in an attacking line, with player 1 in possession of the ball on the left hand side of the grid. Player 1 runs out and makes a pass to player 2 who in turn passes to player 3. Player 2 now runs around behind to take a short pass on the right of player 3. All players run through to the end of the grid.

Coaching points: When performed accurately, this simple skill is very difficult to defend against, and it is important that the coach is constantly on the lookout for good form:

- player 3 must run dead straight to fix the defender.
- player 2 must run the corner tight to player 3 and turn straight upfield, not drift out to take the pass on an angle.

Progression: By introducing a fourth player to the line, player 2 is forced not to drift, as he will end up crowding player 4's space.

CONTACT SKILLS

Having the confidence, strength and control to contest for the ball and hold off defenders while retaining possession of the ball is key in rugby.

The drills in this chapter introduce the role of the tackle shield holder, the safe use of the shield and basic techniques for contact in set situations. They also introduce some easy methods to help players understand the offside rule in a tackle situation and their role in supporting play. Tackling technique is covered in chapter 8, Tackling and Defence.

Young and inexperienced players can panic when faced with a tackle and offload the ball to be gathered by the defending team, or, when tackled, hang on to the ball when on the ground.

Golden rules

1   When the ball carrier is tackled and on the ground, they must release the ball immediately. Holding on to the ball in a tackle situation will result in a penalty to the opposition.
2   For the attacking team the aim is to retain possession of the ball after a tackle has been made and continue with another phase of attacking play.
3   The tackled player should try to present the ball behind them for a supporting player to pick up – if necessary this may mean falling to the ground with their backs facing their try line, or rolling once on the ground, using their body to shield the ball from the defending side.
4   The tackler, or any other defending players coming into the tackle area, must be on their feet before they try and play the ball. They must also approach the ball from their own side, from the back of the feet of their team-mates defending. They cannot join from the side – this is an off-side position and will result in a penalty.

Young players not only need to learn how to use their body in contact situations and continue to build attacking play, they also need to develop their decision-making skills to apply in game play when there are always several different options to consider. This takes time and practise. It is important to build up the complexity of practices slowly when confidence and control are improving.

Try wherever possible to match player sizes so as not to overbear smaller players and provide opportunities for everyone to experience success.

Wales full-back James Hook showing strength and control to hold off the tackle by New Zealand's Adam Thomson and looking to pass the ball.

drill 39 using the tackle shield 1

Objective: To develop safe and efficient skills when using a tackle shield.

Equipment: Two tackle shields per four or six players.

Description: The player inserts their left arm into the two cross loops of the shield with the right arm supporting the bottom of the shield. The left shoulder is braced to the shield ready to accept contact (for a left-handed player the same instructions apply for the right side). The shield carrier leans into the shield with a wide stance side-on so that the weight is over the front left foot. The coach can test the stability of shield carriers by shaking/pushing them. Players with shields face each other, place the face of the shields together and attempt to push the other player backwards. Change shield users and repeat until all players in a team have had a go.

Coaching points: Emphasise the foot positions and the lean into the shield. The shield carriers must understand that they play an important role in any exercise. They must offer a firm, strong platform against which another player can work. The shield must always be kept up vertically, unless otherwise instructed. Shield carriers must absorb every blow, but must not be aggressive.

Progression: Ask players to alternate arms and body positioning when using the shield.

drill 40 using the tackle shield 2

Objective: To develop safe and efficient skills when using a tackle shield.

Equipment: One tackle shield between two players.

Description: Player 1 stands with a tackle shield as described in the previous drill, ready to take contact. Player 2 is kneeling on one knee 2 m from the pad. On the coach's command, player 2 gets up and drives into the pad in an attempt to move it back by 1 m. Stop the drive after a count of three. The shields must put up good resistance and try to hold their ground. Rotate the players so they all get the chance to use the tackle shield, and also be the driver.

Coaching points: By positioning player 2 too close to the shield, there will only be a relatively small amount of momentum from the driving player – this is important while the players gain confidence. Insist on good form – players must resist the temptation to bowl into the pad without any control. Shield carriers must absorb every blow, but must not be aggressive. Player 2 must aim to make contact with the shoulder point, and wrap their arms around the pad.

Progression: Change contact shoulder.

drill 41 taking contact with a ball

Objective: To develop the correct contact technique for a ball carrier.

Equipment: One tackle shield and one ball for every two players.

Description: Player 1 stands with a tackle shield as described in the previous drill, ready to take contact. Player 2 stands 2 m from the shield with a ball. On the coach's command player 2 walks into the shield, keeping the ball away from the shield. If contact is made with the left shoulder, the ball should be under the right arm but secured with the left, and vice versa. Player 1 must put up good resistance and try to hold their ground.

Coaching points: The ball carrier must take the ball in two hands but close to the body. Emphasise the correct body position – the cues are as follows:

- ball away from the shield.
- head up – aim for a spot on the shield to hit.
- hit with the shoulder.
- low hips at the point of contact and drive up and forwards and not down.
- use small steps.

At the point of contact have the player shout 'one, two, three' as they drive. They should aim to get two small driving steps in to every count. The shouting helps inject some energy and controlled aggression to the drill. Rotate the players so they all get the chance to use the tackle shield, and also be the driver.

Progression: As competency increases, increase the speed of the ball carrier but do not allow the ball carrier to run more than three strides into the shield. Change contact shoulder.

taking contact with a ball and a supporting player 1

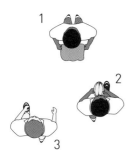

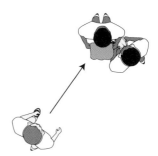

Objective: To develop correct contact technique for a ball carrier.

Equipment: One tackle shield and one ball for every three players.

Description: Player 1 stands with a tackle shield as described in drill 41, ready to take contact. Player 2 stands 2 m from the pad with a ball. On the coach's command, player 2 walks into the pad keeping the ball away from the shield. Player 1 must put up good resistance and try to hold their ground. Player 3 acts as the supporting player – as player 2 makes contact player 3 follows in to secure the ball. Rotate the players so they all get the chance to use the tackle shield, and also be the driver and supporter.

Coaching points: The ball carrier must take the ball in two hands but close to the body. Player 3 must watch which way player 2 hits the shield – if it is with the left shoulder then player 3 should drive in on the ball using his right, protecting the ball from the side. This sounds complex, but it will become the obvious way for player 3 to hide or shield the ball. If he goes in on the wrong shoulder then he cannot make contact with his shoulder as player 2's backside will be in the way and the ball will be there for all to see.

Progression: As competency increases, increase the speed of the ball carrier but do not allow the ball carrier to run more than three strides into the shield. Shield carriers must provide a strong target and absorb the impact, but must not be aggressive.

taking contact with a ball and a supporting player 2

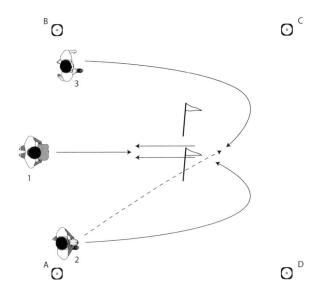

Objective: To improve contact technique for a ball carrier and supporting players; to introduce the concept of offside for a supporting player joining a contact situation.

Equipment: One tackle shield, one ball, two corner flags and four cones for every three players.

Description: Place the cones (A, B, C, D) as shown in the diagram, creating a 3 m by 4 m grid, with two corner flags 1 m infield and 1 m apart forming a 'gate'. Player 1 stands between cones A and B with a tackle shield, ready to take contact. Player 2 (with the ball) and player 3 stand beside player 1, with all three players facing the same direction into the grid. Player 2 rolls the ball out between the flags and player 3 runs to gather the ball before turning to make contact with the pad through the gate. Player 2 runs out with him and turns to act as the supporting player. Both players must go out on the outside of the flags and return through the gate. The shield must put up good resistance and try to hold their ground. Rotate the players so they all get the chance to use the tackle shield, and also be the driver and supporter.

Coaching points: Ensure that the ball is rolled within the grid, therefore restricting the distance the ball carrier can run into the shield. The supporting player must return through the 'gate', ensuring they come from an onside position to join the contact (the idea of a gate at the back of a maul or ruck is one that is often used by referees to indicate where players can join). Ensure that there is good ball protection on impact, and that the supporting player binds with the ball carrier.

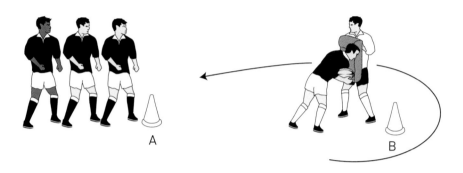

drill 44 — ball retention on contact

A

B

Objective: To accustom players to retain possession of the ball when in contact and going to ground.

Equipment: Two cones, one shield and one ball for every group.

Description: Divide the players into groups of three, four or five. Place the cones 3 m apart. One player stands at cone B with the shield, while the rest of the players stand at cone A in a line. On the coach's command, the first player advances to the shield and gives a loud count of 'one' (drives into the shield), 'two' (drops to the ground protecting the ball), 'three' (lays the ball back with both hands, under control). The player then returns to the team with the ball, which is handed to the next player and the drill is repeated.

Coaching points: The contact must be firm, positive and vigorous. Shield holders must be encouraged to play their part to make a firm base. As the player contacts the shield, the ball must be kept away from the shield, and it must not touch it. When the player falls, the ball must not touch the ground, until it is laid back under complete control.

Progression: A team drill can be developed, with a second player running out as the ball is presented on the count of three, picking it up and running around the shield before returning to the next player to continue.

Objective: To encourage competitive play in a controlled contact environment.

Equipment: None.

Description: Players lie facing each other in pairs, face down on the floor. On the coach's command, players race to get to their feet to try and impede their opponent getting up. They can use any means within the rules of rugby.

Coaching points: This can be developed into a tournament by constantly pairing winners until a 'grand champion' emerges.

Progression: With older/stronger players, start in a press-up position with players facing each other head-to-head. Same rules apply but with option of pulling arms etc.

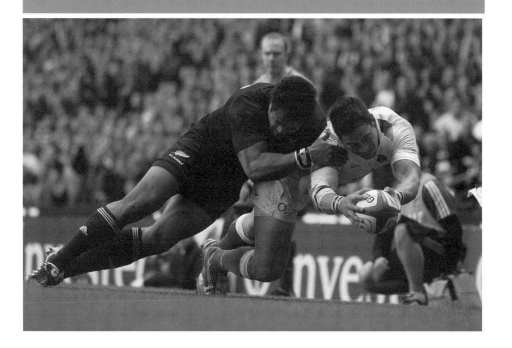

New Zealand's Isaia Toeava makes a try-stopping tackle on England's Shontayne Hape.

drill 46   controlling the ball on impact

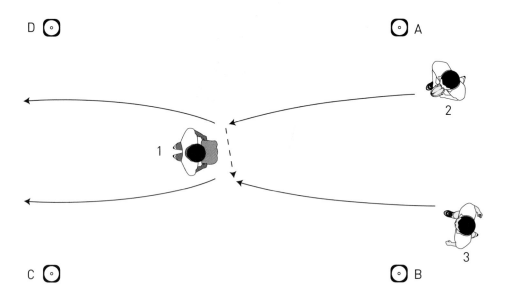

Objective: To develop the correct technique when establishing a ruck.

Equipment: One tackle shield, one ball and four cones for every three players.

Description: Place the cones (A, B, C, D) as shown in the diagram, creating a 3 m × 4 m grid. Player 1 stands in the centre of the grid with a tackle shield, ready to take contact. Players 2 and 3 are at the end of the grid between cones A and B with the ball on the floor just in front of them. On the coach's command, player 2 gathers the ball and then drives into the shield in an attempt to move it back 1 m. After contact, player 2 falls to the floor keeping the ball close and secure, before pushing it out along the floor at arm's length allowing player 3 to pick up and run through to the far cones (C and D) to be joined by player 2. The ball is placed on the floor again, and the drill is repeated with player 3 carrying. Keep rotating the players so they all get a chance to play in the different positions.

Coaching points: Ball carriers must fall with their back to the shield. There must be a defined structure to this process, and you might find it helpful to illustrate this by walking the players through the drill and applying a key word to each phase such as 'hit, drive, down, ball'. There will be a tendency for younger players to flop on the floor and just release the ball. Encourage the players to focus on controlling the ball at all times. Praise players who do not let the ball touch the floor before it is placed back. Players can call out 'hit, drive, down, ball' to help focus.

drill 47   clearing out at the tackle

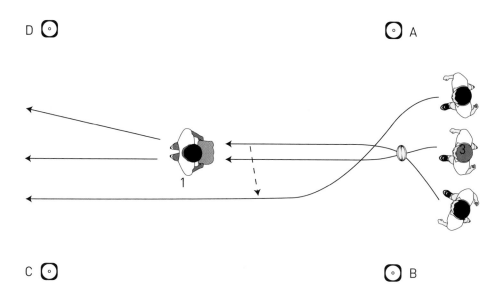

D ⊙   ⊙ A

C ⊙   ⊙ B

Objective: To develop the correct technique when clearing defenders from a tackle situation.

Equipment: One tackle shield, one ball and four cones for every four players.

Description: Place the cones (A, B, C, D) as shown in the diagram, creating a 3 m × 5 m grid. Player 1 stands in the centre of the grid with a tackle shield, ready to take contact. Players 2, 3 and 4 are at the end of the grid between cones A and B, with the ball on the floor just in front of them. On the coach's command, player 2 gathers the ball and then drives into the shield in an attempt to move it back 1 m. As before, player 2 falls to the floor after contact, keeping the ball close and secure. Player 3 steps over player 2 and drives into the shield to clear the tackle area. The ball is then pushed back for player 4 who comes in to pick up the ball and runs through to the far cones (C and D). The ball is placed on the floor again, and the drill is repeated with player 3 carrying. Keep rotating the players so they all get a chance to play in the different positions.

Coaching points: Timing is everything. If player 3 is too late the ball will be lost too soon and the ball carrier will not have gone to ground and there will not be a target to hit. Players 2 and 3 must quickly get away from the contact to support player 4.

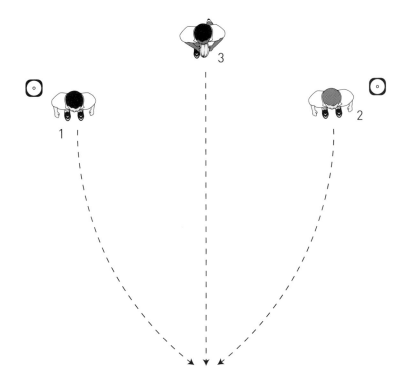

Objective: To develop competition for a loose ball on the floor.

Equipment: Two cones and one ball for every three players.

Description: Place the two cones 1 m apart, with players 1 and 2 positioned on the inside of each of them. Player 3 has the ball. On the coach's command, player 3 rolls the ball between the two players (no more than 3 m). The moment the ball hits the floor, players 1 and 2 compete to secure the ball. Assume that players 1 and 2 are playing in the direction of the arrows. This will help in understanding which way to fall. Each player will try to fall with his back to the arrow.

Coaching points: Try, wherever possible, to match up players by size. Encourage the players to fall hard on the ball, and to position their body between the opposition and the ball. In this way they will be presenting the ball to players who, in a game, will be coming to support. Ball speed and controlled aggression are the keys to success, but do not allow any more wrestling on the ground than would be allowed in a game. The player arriving second is not allowed to fall on the player in possession, but can compete for the ball as long as he stays on his feet.

drill 49

clearing out the tackle – game situation

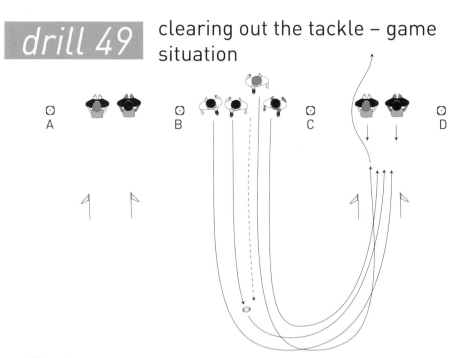

Objective: To simulate clearing defenders from a tackle situation.

Equipment: Four tackle shields, one ball, four corner flags and four cones for every eight players.

Description: Place the cones (A, B, C, D) at 2 m intervals in a line. Four players have tackle shields, and they are set up in tight pairs between cones A/B and C/D with a pair of flags 1 m apart and 1 m in front of each pair to make an 'onside gate'. The remaining players 1–4 stand between cones B/C. The ball is rolled out (no more than 4 m) and player 1 runs out to gather it before turning and driving into one pair of shields (his choice) via a gate, and goes to floor to present the ball as before. As the ball is rolled out, the shields advance one stride to just behind the gates. Players 2 and 3 bind together and drive them out of the way. Player 4 follows up to secure the ball and runs through to complete the drill. Allow plenty of rest and keep rotating the players.

Coaching points: Before the drill starts, emphasise the key points for the shield holders and driving/clearing players. The shields must put up good resistance and try to hold their ground on impact. Ball carriers must fall with their back to the shield. Walk each group through perfect form so that everyone understands before increasing pace. Timing of the arrival at the clearout is vital. Too soon and there is no momentum. Too late and the ball will be lost.

Progression: When competency is established allow more freedom amongst the attackers. Communication is key to the success of this – one player must call for the ball and supporters must talk so everyone knows their role within the drill.

drill 50

competing for the ball on the floor – group skills

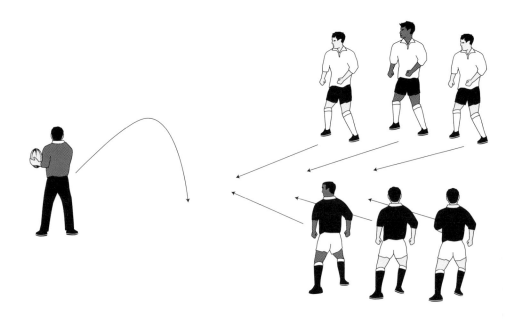

Objective: To develop group competition skills for a loose ball on the floor.

Equipment: One ball for every six players.

Description: Divide the players into teams of three. Each team of three then pairs up to play against each other. Players line up in their teams, 1 m apart and facing in the same direction (as if in a lineout). The coach stands facing the lines (no more than 3 m away) with the ball. The coach throws the ball straight up to around head height. The moment the ball hits the floor the two groups compete to secure the ball.

Coaching points: Try, wherever possible, to match up players by size. Encourage the players to fall hard on the ball, secure it safely and position their body between the opposition and the ball. In this way they will be presenting the ball to players who, in a game, will be coming to support. Ball speed and controlled aggression are the keys to success, but do not allow any more wrestling on the ground than would be allowed in a game. The player arriving second is not allowed to fall on the player in possession but can compete for the ball as long as he stays on his feet. The player on the floor can pass the ball up to supporters if he is not being tackled, and can also roll it back.

drill 51 — clearing out at the tackle – progression

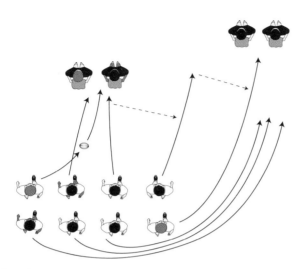

Objective: To improve clearing defenders from a tackle situation.

Equipment: Six tackle shields and one ball for every fourteen players.

Description: Six players have tackle shields, and they are set up in tight pairs in a staggered line as shown, no more than 5 m apart. The attackers (players 1–8) stand 3 m in front of the first pair of shields. The coach drops the ball in front of the attackers, one of whom (player 1) picks up and drives into the first pair of shields. The drill develops as follows:

- Players 2 and 3 drive over to clear out the shields
- Player 4 comes in as dummy half and passes to player 5 who drives into the second pair of shields
- Players 6 and 7 drive the shields away
- Player 8 comes in as dummy half and passes to the supporting players arriving from the previous contact, and continues the drill into the final pair of shields.

Allow plenty of rest and keep rotating the players.

Coaching points: This drill requires all players to have a good understanding of the skills involved, and should not be introduced until the previous drills are clearly understood. Walk the players through the drill and slowly increase the speed. Emphasise the need for players to get back into support quickly after contact is made and to get the ball away. Communication is key to the success of this drill, so players must talk to each other often. Timing is critical, particularly for players taking the pass from the dummy half.

drill 52   pop pass from the tackle

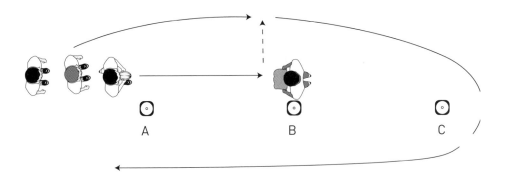

Objective: To introduce the skill of delivering a pop pass from a tackled player on the ground.

Equipment: Three cones, one shield and one ball for every group.

Description: Divide the players into groups of three, four or five. Place the cones in a line, 3 m apart. One player stands at cone B with the shield, while the rest of the players stand at cone A in a line. On the coach's command, the first player runs forwards with the ball, drives into the shield, and falls to the ground protecting the ball. As he falls, the second player from the team runs forwards to his aid. As he arrives, the fallen player on his back delivers a soft upwards pass into the stomach of his oncoming team-mate. The ball is then carried around cone C and back to the team for the drill to be repeated.

Coaching points: The ball must not touch the ground. The tackled player must protect the ball on impact, and must attempt to land on his side, shoulder or back in order to be able to see the oncoming supporter and to deliver the pass. Emphasise that the pass must be careful and delivered accurately into the midriff. On no account must it be a hard pass. The supporting player must time his run, arriving at the pass at maximum speed and carrying on to the next cone.

Progression: When a degree of skill has developed, two players can support the fallen player – one to receive the pop pass and the other to receive a second pass.

drill 53 competitive ball possession

Objective: To accustom young players to compete vigorously but fairly for ball possession.

Equipment: One ball per pair.

Description: Pair up the players, trying to match them by size where possible. These pairs are spread over a teaching area, with one player in possession of the ball. On the coach's command, the other player attempts to wrestle the ball from his partner's grasp. Time the wrestle, starting with 10 seconds. You can increase the time, but do not allow combats to go on too long.

Coaching points: The ball carrier can bend and hide the ball in the midriff. He can also turn away from the tackler, and is allowed to protect his ball vigorously. Body shaking, pushing and even jumping up and down can be permitted under strict controls. The tackler can use any means available under the rules of rugby to win the ball. No hitting is allowed. A useful tip is to drive an arm either up or down between the player's body and the ball.

Progression: When players are used to this exercise, encourage them to push at the same time. The tackler may fight for the ball and at the same time gain ground even though he doesn't win the ball.

LINEOUT

The lineout is a throw-in used to restart the game when a ball is kicked into touch. This important set-piece play requires communication and accuracy of throwing to reach the targeted team member, strength and control in jumping to retrieve the ball, the ability to protect the ball from the opposition and confidence to make the ball available to the scrum-half to continue to attack.

The drills in this chapter look at basic techniques for throwing and catching in a lineout, focusing on accuracy and developing confidence. These drills progress to introduce developing attacking play from a lineout and defensive lineout situations. Build the complexity as confidence and understanding develop and focus on good technique throughout.

Coaching points

1 When being introduced to rugby, all players can practise throwing and jumping techniques – it is not just a hooker who has to pass accurately or the forwards who have to jump!

2 To achieve a well-timed jump, players should hold good body position, with knees and arms slightly bent, and wait for the ball to be thrown. Use of arms and driving up from the knees is important to create an explosive action in the jump.

3 The thrower should seek to match the high point of the path of the throw with the highest point of the jump – not just to land the throw on to the player. Players should aim to catch the ball at the highest point.

4 Encourage players to focus on the seams of the ball, aiming to catch the seams – this helps young players focus on the ball even when excited. Asking players which part of the ball did they catch will help them achieve this.

5 There should be a 1 m gap between both lines and no contact is allowed until the player lands.

Remember, young players (under 16) are not able to support or lift players in the jump at the lineout for safety reasons.

Tom Croft of England contesting for and winning lineout ball from Rocky Elsom of Australia.

drill 54 throwing-in and catching at a lineout

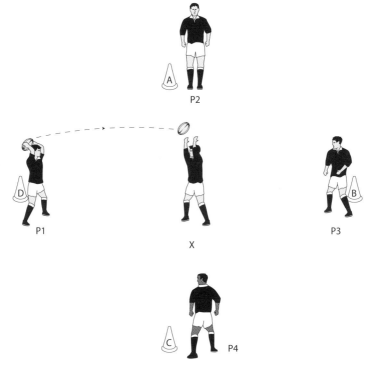

Objective: To introduce the lineout skill of catching a ball above the head.

Equipment: Four cones and one ball for every five players.

Description: Place the cones in a diamond shape as shown, with the outer cones 5 m from the central cone. Players 1–4 stand at cones A–D with a catcher (X) in the middle. The catcher stands with his arms above his head, and player 1 attempts to hit the catcher's hands using a football-style throw-in. The catcher then passes to the next thrower in sequence and the exercise is repeated around the diamond. Then the catcher changes places with the thrower, and the exercise is repeated until all have had a turn at catching.

Coaching points: The catcher should stand with their hands six to eight inches apart, with their palms at about 45 degrees forming a funnel. The emphasis is on relaxed hands – do not grab at the ball. Throwers should experiment with holding the ball across the widest part, or with one hand on the widest part and the other on the rear part.

Progression: On catching the ball, the player turns to the left, pulls the ball down into his waist and bends quickly over the ball to hide it. Try this sequence slowly at first, and as players become more skilful, ask them to turn and bend in one movement.

drill 55 jumping and catching

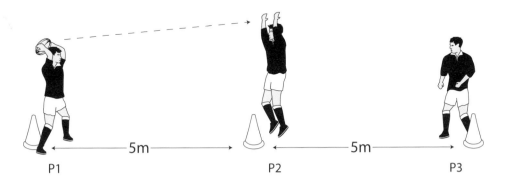

P1   P2   P3

Objective: To develop jumping and catching skills.

Equipment: One ball and three cones for every three players.

Description: Place the cones in a straight line, 5 m apart. One player stands at each cone. Player 1 throws in to player 2, who stands with arms slightly raised. The throw is aimed slightly above the hands of player 2 so that they have to jump to catch it. If the ball goes over player 2, player 3 must catch it, and have a turn at throwing.

Coaching points: The players must have good body positioning with their legs and arms slightly bent. Timing is crucial, and the jump should not be attempted until the ball is in the air. When they catch the ball, the player must land and bend into the ball-protecting position. Rotate the players so that they have all had a turn in each position.

Progression: As specialist jumpers emerge, ask the throwers to test how high the jumper can reach. The ultimate skill is to be able to catch the ball and at the top of the jump using the hands and wrists to flick the ball down to the scrum-half. This is a skill that is rare in young players. It will develop with time, age and experience. Work slowly and carefully on this aspect.

drill 56 passing off the top of the lineout

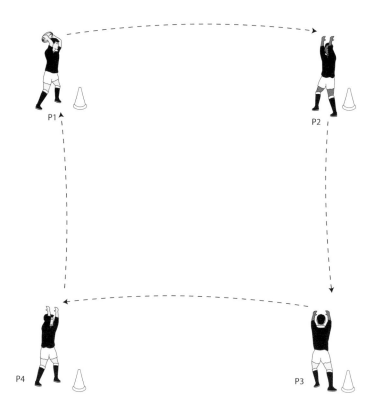

Objective: To develop the pass from the lineout to scrum-half.

Equipment: One ball and four cones for every four players.

Description: Place the cones in a square, with a player positioned at each cone. Player 1 throws the ball as in a lineout for player 2 to catch. After catching the ball, player 2, with his hands still above his head, turns and passes to player 3. Player 3 then throws to player 4 who turns and passes to player 1. Repeat around the square.

Coaching points: This is a difficult skill for young players. Emphasise the need to turn slightly before passing. The pass off the top should aim at the target player's raised hands. The pass will inevitably drop in flight, allowing a good catching opportunity. If aimed at the waist the drop in flight can cause the catcher to bend.

Progression: Catcher bends at the waist to protect the ball and then passes to scrum-half.

drill 57 lineout to maul

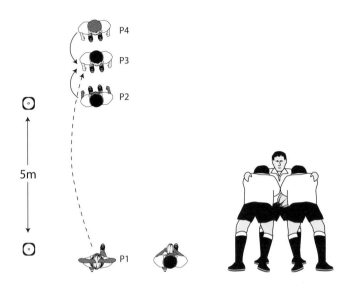

Objective: To develop a system of protecting the ball after the lineout catch.

Equipment: One ball and two cones for every four players.

Description: Players are set out as shown in the diagram. Allow an arm's length between each member of the lineout team. Player 1 throws to player 3 (with raised arms). Player 3 pulls the ball down into his waist and bends, then players 2 and 4 move in to bind around the waist of player 3 (player 2 with right arm and player 4 with left arm). After completion, players 2, 3 and 4 will form a 'V' shape.

Coaching points: Measuring the distance between themselves and the player in front by using an arm's length will prevent over-crowding. Players 2 and 4 must face player 3 during the throw. On contact, the heads of players 2 and 4 must be at waist level. Emphasise good foot positioning with wide stance, toes pointing forwards, knees bent, chin up, flat back and eyes up and open. The bind must be tight, and the ball must be buried out of sight. Rotate the players so that they have all had a turn in each position.

Progression: Add two players with tackle shields to act as opposition for the maul to push against. Player 1 (the thrower) can follow up to take the ball from the back of the maul.

drill 58 five man lineout

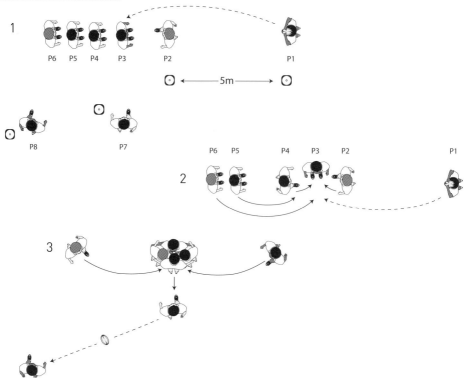

Objective: To develop more player involvement in the lineout.

Equipment: One ball and four cones per team.

Description: Lineout players set out as in diagram. P1 is 5 m from the front of the line with the ball. P7 is 2 m from the lineout as a scrum-half. P8 is 10 m from the line as an outside half. Throw in to P3 who bends and conceals the ball at waist level. P2 and P4 move in and bind to make a V shape. P5 moves in to secure the ball while staying bound with one arm in the pushing position. (This is called 'smuggling'.) P1 and P6 move in and bind onto the two players (P2 and P4) already in position to complete the maul. P7 (the scrum-half) goes into the back of the 'V' between the players to take the ball, which is then passed to P8. Repeat the exercise three to four times, then rotate players.

Coaching points: This is a complicated procedure at first. Play it slowly and then speed up. Emphasise good foot positioning with wide stance, toes pointing forwards, knees bent, chin up, flat back and eyes up and open. Emphasis is on a tight bind and a good pushing position at all times.

Progression: One of the players at the back can slip a binding arm and secure the ball from the catcher and present it back to P8.

drill 59 defensive lineout 1

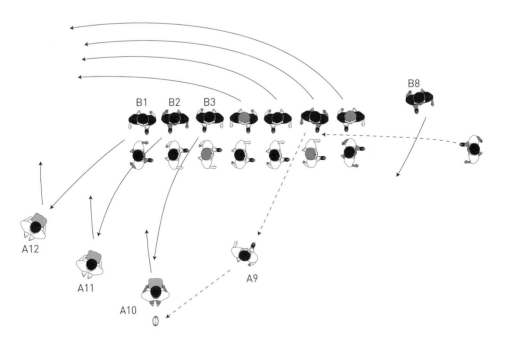

Objective: To develop skills and practices associated with a defensive lineout.

Equipment: One ball, three tackle shields and three cones.

Description: Divide the players into teams, with each team containing two sets of forwards (six or eight a side) and three backs with tackle shields (on the attacking side). The lineout is uncontested and the attacking side wins the ball. It is passed to the scrum-half (A9) who passes slightly behind and as if the ball goes to floor. The drill continues as if the attacking backs are in possession and the ball has been passed to players A10, A11 and A12 who have advanced as if attacking with the ball. The back three defending forwards B1, B2 and B3 leave the lineout and attack the shields in a defensive formation. The defensive hooker (B8) closes around the front of the lineout to block any potential blind side moves by the scrum-half. The remainder of the defensive forwards having determined that the ball is away can support across field. Give each set of forwards a turn.

Coaching points: The defending players must not leave the lineout until the ball has passed from the lineout to the scrum-half. Organisation is needed to allocate defensive roles to the back three players to avoid all three going for the same shield.

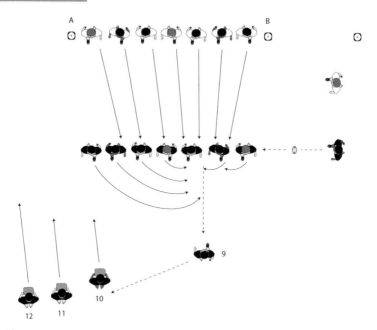

Objective: To accustom players to the skills needed in a defensive lineout.

Equipment: One ball, three tackle shields and four cones.

Description: Divide the players into teams, with each team containing two sets of forwards (six or eight a side), a scrum-half and three backs (on the attacking side). The lineout players must be contained within the two cones A and B, which are 15 m apart. The lineout is uncontested and the attacking side wins the ball. Immediately players bind in around it to set up a maul to protect the ball and the defending side sets up to defend. No push is required at this stage. The ball is smuggled back to the scrum-half (player 9) who passes slightly behind player 10 and the ball goes to floor. The drill continues as if the attacking backs are in possession and the ball has been passed to player 11 and player 12 who have advanced as if attacking. One or more defending forwards must bind on the side of the maul, looking to the opposition to see what is happening. When the ball is released by player 9 the first defender off the side of the maul heads to mid-field with the intention of getting between player 10 and player 12 to make a tackle and disrupt their line.

Coaching points: The offside rule must be observed, players must remain properly bound to the maul, otherwise they must retire behind the back foot of the maul.

Progression: Practise slowly, and gradually increase speed. Begin with an uncontested lineout then graduate to the attacking side being allowed to win the ball but putting in a contested push.

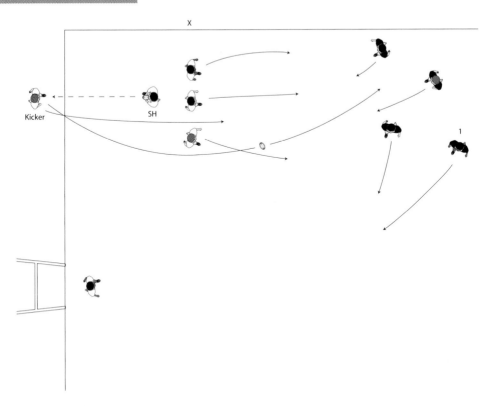

Objective: To emphasise the rules governing being offside in front of the kicker, and to practise attacking and defensive patterns.

Equipment: Eight, nine or ten players – several balls.

Description: Set up three or four players in a lineout at X complete with scrum-half, and side or full-back (kicker). Other players form a reception group 20 m along the touchline. The ball is passed from the lineout to the scrum-half, who passes to the kicker to kick downfield, aiming for touch. The reception group field the ball and start a passing movement back upfield. The lineout forwards move downfield to cut off the impending attack.

Coaching points: The prime objective is to ensure that no lineout player begins a run in front of the kicker before the ball is kicked and he has advanced – emphasise that this is the basis of the offside rule. Change players around and test new kickers. Look for attacking and defending players quickly forming attacking and defending lines after the kick.

Progression: Lineout forwards do not all attack the reception group's ball-carrier; some fan out across the pitch to cut off passes into mid-field.

RUCK, MAUL, SCRUM

Rucks, mauls and scrums are combative, technical aspects of rugby that require strength, controlled aggression and good discipline to enable an attacking team to retain or gain possession of the ball, gaining advantage and territory. Young players must learn the skills and control to enable them to perform these techniques effectively without giving away penalties for breaking the rules.

Rucks

A ruck forms following a tackle when the tackled player releases the ball once they are on the ground. There is a tendency for players (young and old!) to want to hang on to the ball when tackled to allow their team-mates to catch up – this will result in a penalty.

   The aim of the ruck is to try and move a loose ball back to the player's own side. The forwards are usually involved in the ruck and they must only use their feet to move the ball.

Mauls

When a tackled player is held up rather than pulled to the ground a maul may form. In this situation forwards from either side bind on to the ball carrier and each other and, remaining on their feet, they try to work the ball back to their side using their arms and hands.

   In both rucks and mauls the aim is to quickly regain possession of the ball to enable a team to create opportunities for attacking play.

Scrums

The scrum is a set piece which allows a game to restart after an infringement. It involves the eight forwards from each team binding together and trying to push each other backwards in order to gain possession of the ball.

   The formation of a scrum is strictly governed for the safety of the players and discipline is essential to avoid injuries. The drills in this chapter cover the basics of scrummage technique and break these elements down to the component parts. It is important for young players to learn the correct technique from the start; begin slowly and build up the practices as confidence and abilities develop.

   In all these elements of play, focusing on good discipline with young players will help them to form good habits, which will prevent them from giving away possession and potential points because they have failed to follow the rules through frustration or uncontrolled reactions – sometimes easier said than done!

A successful ruck resulting in Chris Cussiter retrieving and clearing the ball for Scotland.

drill 62 pushing position 1

1  3

Objective: To introduce and practise correct techniques for pushing.

Equipment: Players and a wall.

Description: Start with players leaning against a wall with hands a little below chest height and feet back so their body is angled at 45 degrees – see diagram 1. Players walk their hands down the wall, bending their knees as they go. Count to three to hold the position.

Coaching points: Focus on good positioning – this is key for players' safety and worth practicing to develop good technique from the start. Look for a wide stance, toes pointing forwards, knees bent, back flat and chin up with eyes up and open. Watch out for weak, rounded backs – emphasise the strength and safety achieved through a flat, straight back.

Progression: In pairs players face each other on hands and knees and bind in a scrummaging position – see diagram 2. On coach's command players push forwards under control – this will cause them to rise into the pushing position – see diagram 3. Hold for a count of three and return to the start. Repeat the movement to give players confidence in a controlled environment.

Remember the correct body position at all times. The move can be broken down into two stages:

1 **squeeze** – the player squeezes everything tight, braces the chest and pulls the belly button in (this helps protect the back and keep it flat throughout the move) and pulls the bind tight.
2 **up** – the player pushes forwards and up, retaining tension in their chest and core, pushing off the ground with their toes.

Watch for players rounding their backs as they push off the ground. Players can keep a hand on the ground to start until a consistent correct technique is achieved.

pushing position 2

Objectives: To develop the skill of pushing with a dynamic exercise.

Equipment: One tackle shield for every two players.

Description: Divide the players into pairs. One player holds the shield and the other player adopts the pushing position by wrapping their arms around the shield. Players must walk their legs backwards to achieve the correct position, and hold for a count of three. Players then change position so they both have a chance to use the shield. There should be no forward movement.

Coaching points: Emphasise good positioning with wide stance, toes pointing forwards, knees bent, chin up, flat back and eyes up and open. Watch out for rounded backs – this is a weak position and needs to be avoided – and emphasise the need for a straight spine. Ensure that the shoulder of the pusher is solidly in contact with the shield, and instruct the shield carriers to provide a solid platform against which to push – without this solid platform the pusher will fall down.

Progression: Line up the shields, and stand behind the line of shields providing a hand signal for the pushers to stop. This requires the players to look up.

drill 64   binding and pushing

Objective: To develop the team skills to push in a scrummage.

Equipment: Two tackle shields for every four players and four cones.

Description: Divide the players into two sets of pairs, and place the cones in a 3 m grid. Two players take up tackle shields and stand shoulder-to-shoulder between the top two cones. A second pair of players (pushers) stands facing them between the bottom two cones, shoulder-to-shoulder with their inside arms around each other's waists. Pushers step forwards to the shields and bend into a pushing position – the player on the right puts his head into the gap between the two shields. Their arms should be bound around the shield firmly, and their shoulders are in contact with the shield. On the coach's command, the pushers must attempt to push the shields backwards, but no more than half a metre. Try two or three repetitions, then change shield carriers.

Coaching points: Emphasise the correct body position as shown in the previous three drills. Take this exercise in slow stages and watch carefully how individuals are reacting. Step in quickly if there is any twisting or danger of falling. Pushers must work together as a pair and be firmly bound around each other's waist. Ensure that shield carriers play their part, giving a firm upright stable platform. They should retreat slightly on the push but maintain good pressure on the pushers – they are there to help the players develop good pushing skills, not to drive them back.

drill 65 front row structure

Objective: To develop the skills of a scrum front row.

Equipment: Three tackle shields, four cones and one ball for every six players.

Description: Divide the players into two sets of three, and place the cones in a 3 m grid. Three players take up tackle shields and stand shoulder-to-shoulder between the top two cones. The other three players stand facing them between the bottom two cones, with the two outside players (props) binding around the waist of the middle player (hooker). The hooker binds across the backs/ shoulders of the two props, gripping their jerseys. On the coach's command, they step forward to the shields – the middle player puts their head into the left gap between the shields and the right hand player puts their head into the right gap. The shoulders of all three pushers make contact with the shields. Pushers move their feet backwards and hold against the shields. The two outside players bind strongly around the shields. On the 'bend' command they bend knees; on the 'push' command they straighten knees and attempt to push the shields backwards. Repeat two or three times, then change players.

Coaching points: Emphasise the correct body position as shown in the previous drills. Players with the shields should have a wide, strong stance. This is important in order to provide a strong, continuous base for the pushing players.

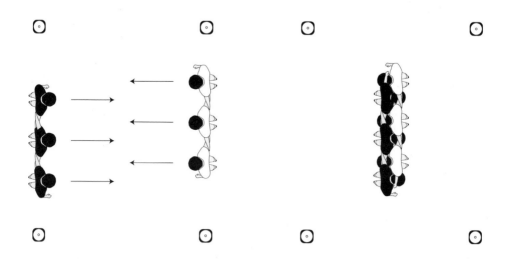

Objective: To develop the skills of two front rows operating in contact.

Equipment: Four cones and one ball for every six players.

Description: Divide the players as shown, inside the cones in a 2 m grid. The players stand in two rows facing each other. Players follow the coach's commands:

- **'crouch'** – both rows bend at the waist (an arm's length apart) and prepare to make contact.
- **'hold'** – they wait.
- **'engage'** – they make contact using correct body positions.

(The top row is deemed to have possession of the ball, therefore the heads of the opposition fit into the gaps as shown in the above diagram.)

- **'push'** – the two rows lean on each other for a count of three.
- **'stop'** – the two rows break up.

Repeat slowly three or four times to accustom players to the experience.

Coaching points: Emphasise the correct body position: a wide stance and feet at 45 degrees, the soles of boots on the ground to give better traction. Bend the knees to lower body height, keep chin up, push chest through for a flat back, eyes open looking for the ball. Knees must not come forwards under the body. They must be kept well back to allow the spine to straighten and deliver the push from the knees.

drill 67 the expanded scrummage 1

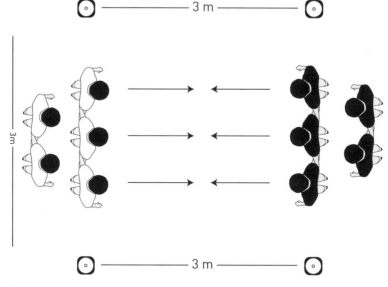

Objective: To develop skills, strength and experience to compete in a five-player scrummage.

Equipment: Four cones and one ball for every ten players.

Description: Divide the players into two sets of five, and place the cones in a 3 m grid. The players stand in two rows facing each other, with three players at the front and two players behind. Players follow the coach's commands:

- **'bind'** – the front rows bind as in drill 66. The two players behind (the locks) bind around each other's waists.
- **'crouch'** – the front rows bend, the two locks remain standing.
- **'touch'** – the front row extends their arms to contact the opposition.
- **'engage'** – the front rows move forwards and lock into position.
- **'lock'** – the two locks insert their heads between the hips of the front row. The locks bind strongly around the buttocks of the players in front.
- **'lean'** – the two scrums lean into each other.

Repeat three of four times, slowly and using the command sequence, to accustom players to the experience.

Coaching points: Emphasise the correct body position: wide stance and feet at 45 degrees, the soles of boots on the ground to give better traction. Bend the knees to lower body height, keep chin up, push chest through for a flat back, eyes open looking for the ball. Knees must not come forwards under the body. They must be kept well back to straighten spine and deliver the push from the knees. Binding is a vital part of the process, and its importance must be emphasised. Locks can grab the jersey of their props to generate a strong link.

drill 68   the expanded scrummage 2

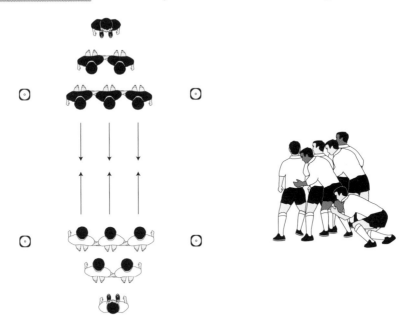

Objective: To develop skills, strength and experience to compete in a six-player scrummage.

Equipment: Four cones and one ball for every twelve players.

Description: When a degree of confidence and skill has been attained in the five-player scrummage in drill 67, two players can be added (No. 8s) to bind onto the two locks, following the same instructions as in drill 67. Practise in sets of three uncontested scrums to start – then introduce a push when it is felt appropriate.

Coaching points: The same points are valid for the no. 8s as for the locks and props – a wide stance and feet positioned at 45 degrees. The soles of boots should be on the ground as much as possible to give better traction. Bend the knees to lower body height, keep chin up, push chest through to get a flat back, eyes open looking for the ball. Knees must not come forwards under the body. They must be kept well back to allow the spine to straighten and deliver the push from the knees. The no. 8s can also bind through the splayed legs of the locks and grasp the fronts of their jerseys. This gives a good pushing position as it automatically brings the no. 8s' shoulders into the correct position on the props' buttocks.

Progression: When the players are ready to progress, the scrum-half gives a signal for the concerted push. On the words 'ball in' the players bend their knees. On the word 'now' they lower their hips and straighten their spine, and straighten their legs to push. Do not allow any push to go further than 1.5 m, or turn more than 45 degrees.

setting a scrummage in a controlled game environment

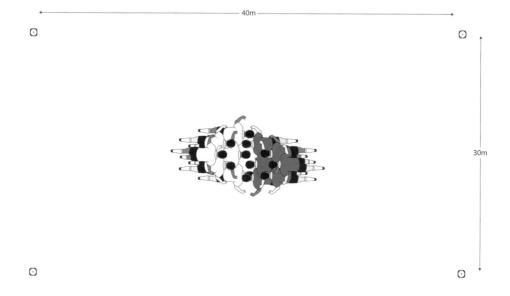

Objective: To develop skills, strength and experience to compete in a full scrummage, and to provide a clearly understood and ingrained routine.

Equipment: Four cones and one ball for every twelve players.

Description: Use the cones to mark a playing area approximately 30 m x 40 m. This drill uses the skills already learned, but in a less structured environment, so that the packs have to learn to operate as a unit. The coach calls for a scrum and makes a mark. The two front rows bind together and then stand on it, an arm's length apart. The second rows bind into a pushing position. The no. 8s then kneel on one knee behind them and bind into place. On the 'crouch' command, the forwards take a pushing position and wait for the 'engage' command. They do not push. Repeat the exercise, resetting the packs in different areas of the playing area.

Progression: When you are satisfied that the skill level is high enough, scrum halves can be added using a ball for uncontested scrums. The next stage is to allow the hookers to compete for the ball with scrums pushing. Encourage the no. 8s to control the ball at their feet. Do not allow any push to go further than 1.5 m or turn more than 45 degrees.

TACKLING AND DEFENCE

Tackling is another physically challenging part of the game involving full contact between players. A tackle is a way for the defending team to try to stop the attacking team gaining territory and advancing toward their try line. The aim of the tackle is to grab hold of the player with the ball and bring them to the ground – once tackled and on the ground a player must immediately release the ball.

Young players need to learn how to tackle correctly (to keep themselves and opponents safe), how to react if tackled and the importance of supporting the tackled player. A successful team is able to retain possession of the ball after being tackled to set up subsequent phases of attacking play.

In this chapter there are drills to practise the basic technique for safe tackling. Correct use of the tackle shield and the role of the shield holder are covered in the chapter 5, Contact Skills.

Young and inexperienced players need to be able to understand the component parts of the tackle and what is required physically – it is important to practise good, basic technique from the start. Coaches can select the level of drill to use depending on the experience and ability of their players. The emphasis is still on having fun and the drills are designed to reinforce the skills needed in these key areas through repetition in different situations. The coach should focus on quality throughout.

Golden rules

1 Only a player with the ball can be tackled – young players need to learn to time the tackle to hit the ball carrier while they still have possession of the ball. If they hit when the pass has been made the tackle is late and a penalty will be awarded against them.
2 A barge is not a tackle! Younger players who may lack confidence and co-ordination, or who are just bigger players, can start tackling by trying to just barge their target to the ground. If a tackler makes no attempt to wrap their arms around the ball carrier it is considered dangerous and will be penalised.
3 The tackle must be made with the hold below the shoulders – a hold any higher is a high tackle and can be dangerous for the person being tackled, which will result in a penalty.
4 A tackler cannot pick up the ball carrier and 'dump' them on the ground. The body of the ball carrier must not turn past horizontal – this is called 'spear' tackling and is another dangerous move that would result in a penalty.

Objective: To introduce the skills required for an effective side-on tackle.

Equipment: Two cones and one ball for every eight players; targets on both thighs of every player.

Description: Divide the players into two teams of four. Each team must line up behind a cone, with the groups at right angles to each other as shown. On the coach's command, player 1 walks out briskly with the ball. Player 2 (the tackler) approaches and executes a side-on tackle. The two players then regain their feet, and run to the end of the opposite line. Players 3 and 4 repeat the drill. When all players have participated, swap sides so that the tackle is executed with the opposite shoulder.

Coaching points: In the approach, instruct the tacklers to keep their head and hands up, and aim for the target sticker on the players' thighs. At the point of contact they should hit and wrap hard with the arms. The attacking player is relatively passive during this introductory phase. Do not allow fends or stepping.

Progression: As skills develop, ask attackers to gradually increase their speed to a jog, half pace, etc.

drill 71 chasing tackles

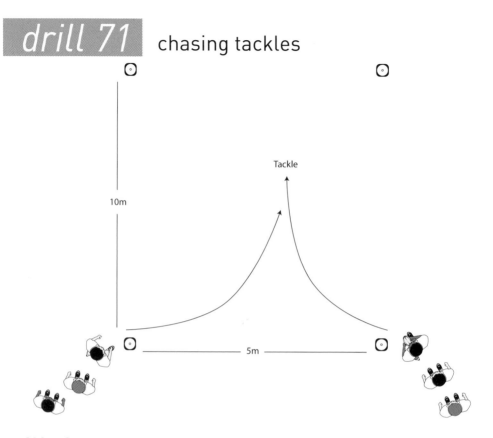

Objective: To introduce the skills required for an effective chase-down tackle.

Equipment: Four cones and one ball for every eight players; targets on both thighs of every player.

Description: Divide the players into two teams of four, and place the cones forming a grid 5 m wide × 10 m long, as shown in the diagram. Each team must line up behind a cone in two parallel lines, and stand approximately 1 m apart. On the coach's command, player 1 walks out briskly with the ball. On the second command, player 2 (the tackler) approaches and executes a tackle from the rear. The two players then regain their feet, and run to the end of the opposite line. Players 3 and 4 repeat the drill. When all players have participated, swap sides so that the tackle is executed with the opposite shoulder.

Coaching points: In the approach, instruct the tacklers to keep their head and hands up, and aim for the target sticker. At the point of contact they should hit and wrap hard with the arms making firm contact and allowing the legs to drag. The tackle should be slightly from the side rather than directly behind. The attacking player is relatively passive during this introductory phase.

Progression: As skills develop, ask attackers to gradually increase their speed to a jog, half pace, etc.

drill 72 head-on tackles game

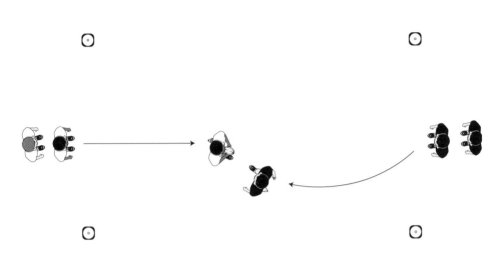

Objective: To introduce the skills required for an effective head-on tackle.

Equipment: Four cones and one ball for every eight players; targets on both thighs of every player.

Description: Divide the players into two teams of four, and place the cones forming a grid 5 m wide × 10 m long, as shown in the diagram. Each team line up between the cones at either end of the grid. On the coach's command, player 1 walks briskly down the centre of the grid with the ball. Player 2 (the tackler) approaches in an arc to force player 1 towards the side of the grid, and then executes a tackle. The two players then regain their feet, and run to the opposite end of the grid to join the back of the line. Players 3 and 4 repeat the drill.

Coaching points: It is important that the tackler approaches in an arc to limit the opportunity for the attacker to evade. Instruct the tacklers to keep their head and hands up, and aim for the target sticker, allowing the legs to drag. The head must go past the thigh or hip, then at the point of contact they should hit and wrap hard with the arms, allowing the legs to drag. The attacking player is relatively passive during this introductory phase. Do not allow fends or stepping.

Progression: As skills develop, ask attackers to gradually increase their speed to a jog, half pace, etc.

drill 73   defensive alignment 1

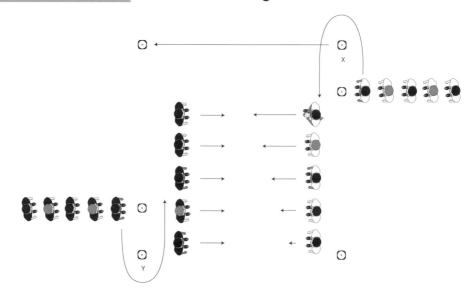

Objective: To create a well-structured defensive line from broken play; to develop defensive communication.

Equipment: Six cones and one ball for every eight players.

Description: Divide the players into two teams of four. Set out a 10 m × 10 m grid using four cones, and place two cones 2 m apart on the left boundary. Both teams line up behind their cones (forming the attack and defence) with the ball on cone X. On the coach's command, both attackers and defenders run from the start point around cone X and Y respectively to form an attacking and defensive line. As the attackers round their cone they pick up the ball. Start the drill at a brisk walking pace with the emphasis on communication. The drill is completed when the attack either completes or is broken down.

Coaching points: Defence – there will be a temptation for the first defensive player to run blindly to the far side of the grid, leaving a gap on the inside. Defenders joining the line must make the outside man aware of their presence, allowing him to push out. By joining in the line from the inside, the attacking run made close to the point of breakdown is always defended.

Attack – as attackers will be joining from the side again there is a temptation to take the ball and set off at a 45-degree angle. This will allow the defenders to drift out and will eventually run the attack out of space. Encourage attackers arriving at the breakdown to straighten the line of running to 'fix' the defenders. The timing of runs is important – too early and the only way to go is sideways, which allows defenders to drift out.

Progression: As competence grows increase the pace.

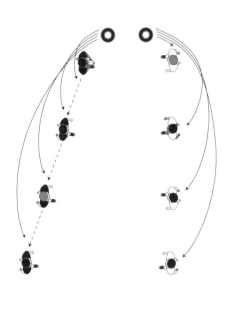

Objective: To create a well-structured defensive line from broken play; to practise attacking from a breakdown and develop communication.

Equipment: Four cones, two tyres and one ball for every eight players.

Description: Divide the players into two teams of four. Set out a 15 m × 15 m grid using the cones, with two tyres 2 m apart in the centre of one side as shown in the diagram – the tyres represent a breakdown and the two extremes of a ruck, and therefore the offside line for the defenders. Both teams group behind their tyre, and the ball is placed in the attackers' tyre. On the coach's command, both attackers and defenders run from the start point to form an attacking and defensive line. Start the drill at a brisk walking pace with the emphasis on communication. The drill is completed when the attack either completes or is broken down.

Coaching points: Follow the same defence and attack points outlined in drill 73.

Progression: As competence grows increase the pace and increase numbers of players to five per side.

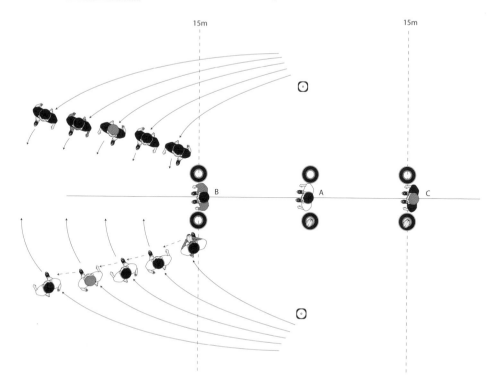

Objective: To create a well-structured defensive line from broken play; to practise attacking from a breakdown.

Equipment: Two cones, six tyres and three balls for every ten to fourteen players.

Description: Divide the players into two teams of between five and seven. On the 22 m line set two tyres 2 m apart in the centre (A) and two on either 15 m line (B and C). Place two cones 10 m out from the centre tyres (the tyres represent a breakdown and the two extremes of a ruck, and therefore the offside line for the defenders). The two teams (defenders and attackers) group behind the cones, and put a ball in each pair of tyres as per the diagram. On the coach's command ('A', 'B' or 'C'), the attackers run to the designated tyre and start an attacking move from that point. The defenders run to form a defensive line at the same tyre while remaining onside. The attackers can choose the right or left side of their breakdown as the point to attack. The drill is completed when the attack either completes or is broken down.

Coaching points: Ensure that the distances between the 'breakdowns' is in keeping with the age of the players – it's a short, sharp drill, not a stamina run!

drill 76 defensive line 1

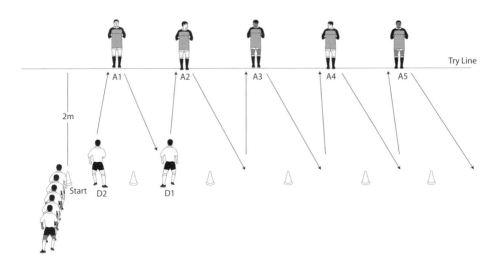

Objective: To introduce defensive alignment.

Equipment: Five tackle shields (each with a target sticker) and six cones for every twelve players.

Description: Divide the players into five attackers and seven defenders. Stand the attackers along the try line at 3 m intervals, each with a tackle shield. Set a line of cones 2 m opposite to create five channels. Defenders line up behind the start cone. On the coach's command, defender 1 (D1) jogs from the start cone to tackle attacker 1 (A1) – he then quickly recovers and moves back and right to 'mark' attacker 2. Defender 2 then steps in opposite attacker 1, and on the coach's command both players move up together and perform a tackle on their respective attackers. The drill continues until there are five defenders moving up in a line. At this point D1 is at the end of the line, and so moves off the grid and returns to the start. In this way the drill can run continuously.

Coaching points: The objective is for the line to move up together. Initially the coach calls the start of the movement, but as understanding grows the player on the left of the drill can call (as this is the point closest to where the ball would be coming from). Ensure that although defenders have to be aware of one another, they have to also concentrate on the tackle skills introduced in previous drills. Tacklers: remember – hands up, heads up, hit the target and wrap with strong arms. Keep rotating attackers and defenders.

Progression: Greater speed can be introduced, but never at the expense of a cohesive line.

Objective: To practise defensive alignment as a group.

Equipment: Five tackle shields (each with a target sticker) and two cones for every ten players.

Description: Divide the players into five attackers and five defenders. Stand the attackers along the try line at 2 m intervals, each with a tackle shield. Defenders line up opposite the attackers on the 5 m line. The coach stands behind the line of defenders facing the attacking line. When the coach puts a hand out to the right or left, the attacking line shuffles sideways on their line in the direction indicated and the defenders must follow them. When the coach puts both hands in the air, the attacking line jogs forwards as if in attack, the defenders advance together in a line and hit their shield as if to make a tackle. Both lines then retire to the starting position and the drill continues. Only when the attackers advance does the defensive line move up.

Coaching points: The idea is to move the defensive line around to challenge communication and therefore coordination. The defensive line must move together to mark their opposite number. There is a lot going on for the defenders but keep emphasising the tackle cues – head up, hands up, spot the target, hit and wrap.

Progression: Greater speed can be introduced, but never at the expense of a cohesive line.

drill 78 defensive line 3

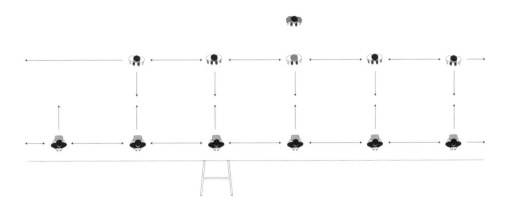

Objective: To improve defensive alignment as a group.

Equipment: Six tackle shields (each with a target sticker) and two cones for every 11 players.

Description: Divide the players into six attackers and five defenders. Stand the attackers along the try line at 2 m intervals, each with a tackle shield. Defenders line up opposite the attackers on the 5 m line (the extra attacker will be the overlap). As in drill 77, the coach stands behind the line of defenders facing the attacking line and signals left, right or advance. The challenge for the defenders is to cope with the overlap attacker by drifting on to the outside player. This is done by initially lining up attacker 1–defender 1; attacker 2–defender 2 etc. with attacker 6 as the overlap. As the coach calls the attack to the right, the defenders must shift to mark one player in the line (defender 1–attacker 2; defender 2–attacker 3 etc.). As before, the coach moves the attack both left and right, until he calls the advance and the tackles are made. Then both teams retire and the drill is repeated.

Coaching points: The idea is to move the defensive line around to challenge communication and co-ordination. The defensive line must move together to ensure that no excessive gaps are left in the line. Encourage lots of talking – in a game situation the players on the inside must constantly communicate with the defenders outside them. This allows the defence to drift without having to keep checking that the inside defenders are in place. There is a lot going on for the defenders but keep emphasising the tackle cues – head up, hands up, spot the target, hit and wrap.

Progression: Greater speed can be introduced, but never at the expense of a cohesive line.

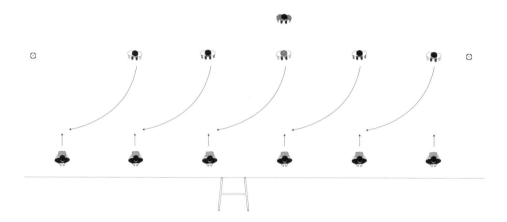

Objective: To develop defensive alignment as a group in a close-to-live situation.

Equipment: Six tackle shields (each with a target sticker) and two cones for every eleven players.

Description: Divide the players into six attackers and five defenders. Stand the attackers along the try line at 2 m intervals, each with a tackle shield. Defenders line up opposite the attackers at a distance of 10 m, and there is an overlap attacker as in drill 78. As before, the coach stands behind the line of defenders and signals left, right and advance. As before, the coach moves the attack both left and right until he calls the advance and the tackles are made. As the defensive team is further away, when the attack comes in the defensive team comes straight up together on the coach's command and drifts out together to cope with the overlapping attacker.

Coaching points: The defence are not able to drift out as this will create gaps on the inside. This drill imitates the situation where the first player is in possession and is marked until he passes, and then the defensive line moves up and out. Encourage lots of talking – in a game situation the players on the inside must constantly communicate with the defenders outside them. This allows the defence to drift without having to keep checking that the inside defenders are in place. There is a lot going on for the defenders but keep emphasising the tackle cues – head up, hands up, spot the target, hit and wrap.

Progression: Replace the coach's command with a call from the inside defender who can now choose when the 'pass' has been made, and calls the drift.

KICKING AND FIELDING

Kicking, if executed properly, can be a potent attacking weapon, but too often it is seen as a purely defensive measure and gives the opposition possession. Most young players, if left on their own, will end up kicking the ball to each other and it's a skill that will be readily received by the players.

There are professional coaches that spend all their lives studying the intricacies of the kicking game and there are many refinements to technique; this section is concerned with the basics of kicking and of defending against kicks.

drill 80 introducing kicking

Objective: Building confidence and competence in a basic kicking technique.

Equipment: Players in pairs with a ball between two.

Description: Players start 5 m apart, facing each other. Focusing on consistent technique, the players kick the ball to each other. The aim is accuracy and the catcher should not have to move.

Coaching points: Hold the ball around its fattest part almost upright, the top leaning towards the catcher. From a standing position (no run up at all) pick up the kicking foot and kick smoothly through the ball. Toes pointed throughout. Place great emphasis on the follow through – have the players pause at the end of the kick, leg straight and toes pointed. Aim to kick the point of the ball and follow through directly at the catcher. The flight should be quite flat, like a pass.

Keep watching the point of contact throughout (this will keep the player's head down and stop them leaning backwards). This is a quiet, relaxed drill – concentration can be helped if the coach asks the players to describe the sound of the kick, the feel of the contact and see the point at which the boot strikes the ball. Don't over coach players new to this skill – let them experiment. Trial and error is a great teacher!

Progression: As confidence builds move the players apart to 10 m, then 15 m, etc. Do not extend the distance at the cost of accuracy. Have the players alter the angle of the ball – what does that do to the flight of the ball? By turning up the toes at the point of contact a higher trajectory can be achieved.

drill 81 develeloping kicking

A

B

C

Objective: Developing techniques for a range of kicks.

Equipment: Players in pairs with a ball between two.

Description: Players start 5 m apart facing each other. Focusing on consistent technique, the players kick the ball to each other. The players alternate between a chip kick (A), flat kick (B) and a grubber kick (C). The aim is accuracy and the catcher should not have to move.

Coaching points: For the chip and flat kick hold the ball as in the previous drill. The chip should see the toes point up and the flat kick the toes point down. For the grubber kick drop the ball on to the foot aiming to kick the ball end over end into the ground about halfway towards the target. For this kick keep the knee over the foot at the point of contact.

Progression: As confidence builds move the players apart to 10 m, then 15 m, etc. Do not extend the distance at the cost of accuracy. Have the kicking player execute the kick walking, then jogging, then running. Aim for perfect execution before progression. Remember: 'Practice doesn't make perfect; it makes permanent! So perfect practice always.' Speed up the drill as skills develop then replace the bags with a live defensive line.

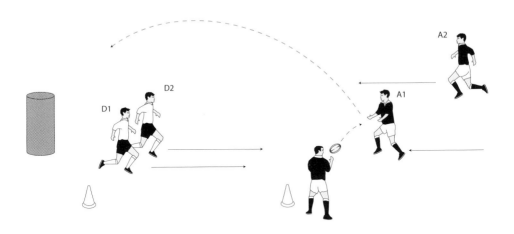

Objective: To develop kicking skills on the run.

Equipment: Two defenders, two attackers, a scrum-half, balls and a tackle bag or shield.

Description: Place the cones 3 m apart to signify the back feet of a ruck or maul. Defenders (D1 and D2) establish a defensive line with the tackle bag 5 m behind them as the target for the kicking player. Attacker one (A1) is passed the ball from the scrum-half feeder as from a ruck or maul. A1 runs onto the ball and kicks through to hit the target bag. The kick can vary from a grubber kick or a chip. Attacker two (A2) runs in support to gather the kick.

Coaching points: Accuracy is the objective, so build the pace gradually. The aim is to hit the bag. If A1 does not move onto the ball he will not encourage the attackers to advance – the run must provide interest for the defenders. Encourage the defenders to defend as if the kick is not necessarily expected – this drill is for the attackers! A2 should adjust the angle and timing of his run to put pressure on the catcher (in this case the target bag) without straying offside. Rotate the players after three turns each.

Progression: Initially the defenders advance slowly providing only shape to the drill. As skills improve have the defenders move at near match pace aiming to pressurise the kick. As a final variation, A1 can have the option to pass to A2 if the defenders are leaving him unmarked and focusing too much on the kicker.

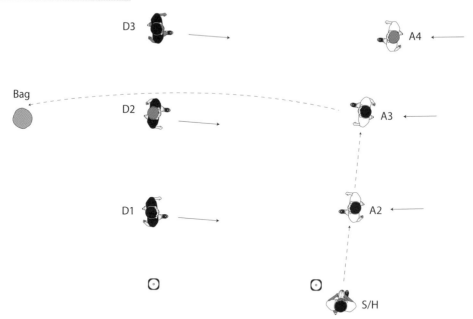

Objective: To develop kicking skills on the run in a game situation; to provide an environment for attacking chasers to time runs.

Equipment: Three defenders, four attackers, a scrum-half (feeder) and balls.

Description: Place the cones 3 m apart to signify the back feet of a ruck or maul. Defenders 1, 2 and 3 establish a defensive line. Attacker two (A2) is passed the ball from the scrum-half feeder as from a ruck or maul. Attacker three (A3) receives the ball and kicks through to hit the target bag. The kick can vary from a grubber kick or a chip. Attackers 2 and 4 (A2 and A4) run to chase and gather the kick.

Coaching points: Accuracy is the objective, so build the pace gradually. The timing of the outside runners is vital to the effectiveness of this skill – A2 must move onto the ball or he will not encourage the attackers to advance. When he receives the ball A2 must be facing the inside shoulder of D1. A3 should start in a conventional attacking line and advance to take a flat pass. A2 and A4 must time their run to ensure that they remain onside but break the line at enough pace to be in a position to pressurise the receiver (who in this drill is represented by the tackle bag). Rotate one player after two turns until everyone has had a go.

Progression: Initially the defenders advance slowly providing only shape to the drill. As skills improve have the defenders move at near match pace aiming to pressurise the kick. As a final variation A3 can have the option to pass to A2 or A4 if the defenders are leaving him unmarked and focusing too much on the kicker.

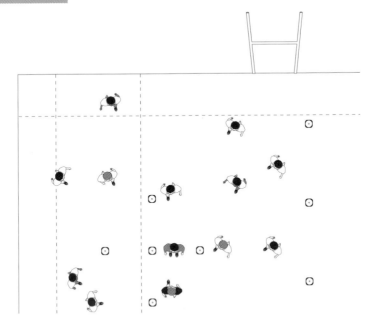

Objective: To challenge the kicker's awareness of space.

Equipment: Five cones and one ball for twelve or more players.

Description: You need at least 12 players for this drill – three are kickers and the rest are fielders with the coach as the bowler. Create a baseball/rounders diamond placing the cone bases 10 m apart with a fifth cone for the 'bowler'. The outfield should be restricted and is best created by using a corner of the pitch, with touchline and tryline as two sides and cones marking out the other boundaries. The coach throws or rolls the ball to kicker 1 who gathers the ball and then immediately kicks into the outfield. Kicker 1 is allowed to keep running as long as the ball has not been fielded. The player is out if caught on the full or 'stumped' on a base (as in rounders) or if the ball goes over the touchline on the full or the dead-ball line.

Coaching points: Once the players have the concept, the coach can use the feed to kicker 1 to test the skill of dispatching the kick quickly. Fielders must communicate to call for the ball clearly and early. Encourage the kicker to aim their kick into a specific space. You may have to adapt the area in which you work to suit the ability of the players.

Progression: Encourage fielders (defenders) to work off the ball. Add a rule that the kicker can only be stopped by the ball being passed through three pairs of hands. This replicates the environment of a back-three supporting a catcher and preparing to counter-attack.

Objective: Developing the skills and techniques for an effective attacking kick.

Equipment: Four players, one ball, cones.

Description: The game is played over the crossbar and into the in-goal area and an equidistant line infield. The teams face each other and chip the ball over the bar with the objective of landing the ball in the opponent's area. The ball must be returned from the point where it is caught.

Coaching points: This is all about kicking into space. The players will have to work to develop angles. Keep repeating the coaching points from the drills – focus on quality.

Progression: The players can use a kick to pass to each other once (more like volleyball) before returning the kick.

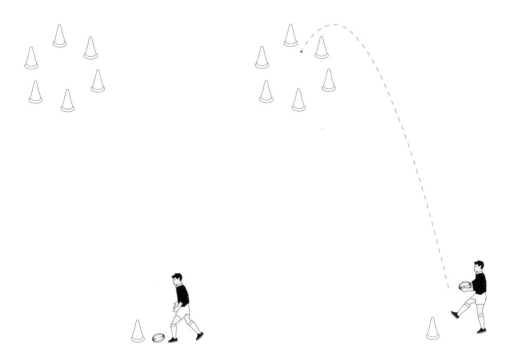

Objective: To introduce the mechanics of the scrum-half attacking 'box kick' (height and accuracy are key as this kick will be used in games to allow team-mates the opportunity to re-gather the ball).

Equipment: Six target cones, one cone and one ball per player (more if possible).

Description: The target cones are placed in a circle as a target grid to land the ball. This grid will vary in size depending on age and competence – start with a big grid (10 m diameter). The kickers set up one cone each about 15 m away from the target circle. The kickers then practise a lobbed box kick into the centre circle. Completed kicks are re-gathered by the players and the drill continues.

Coaching points: Place the ball just behind the cone, and ask the right-footed kicker to take up a wide stance with left foot close to the ball. Reach out for the ball and in one movement the left foot steps away to in front of the right and the kick is executed. By swiftly moving the left foot from the ball to in front of the right, room is created for the kick and the need for a backswing is removed, all of which gains time for successful execution.

drill 87 scrum-half box kick 2

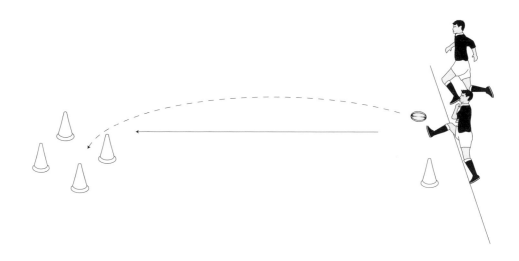

Objective: To develop the mechanics of the scrum-half attacking 'box kick'; to coordinate the run of the chasing winger.

Equipment: Five cones and as many balls as possible for every pair.

Description: In each pair one player is the scrum-half, and one player is the winger. Set up one cone to represent the rear foot of a scrum/maul. The remaining four cones act as a target grid to land the ball. To gauge how far away the grid has to be, time how long the ball stays in the air from the scrum-half's kick and then measure how far the winger can run in that time. This kick can be used as a defensive clearance but it will be useful to provide context by setting the drill up in an attacking field position, e.g. at the intersection of the 15 m and 10 m lines. Taking the cue from the scrum-half's approach to the ball, the winger times his run so that he is running at full tilt and just onside when the ball is kicked. Keep rotating wingers so that quality stays high, and practise on both the left and right sides of the pitch.

Coaching points: The aim is for the winger to arrive at the same time as the ball, but this will take some adjustment by the runner to time their run perfectly. Ask resting players to silently critique the working players, which will increase awareness of the skills and help the development of self-coaching. Vary the points on the pitch where this is executed so that the players can see what works and what does not.

Progression: Introduce a defensive and attacking back row to pressurise the kicker. Only do this once the drill is well understood.

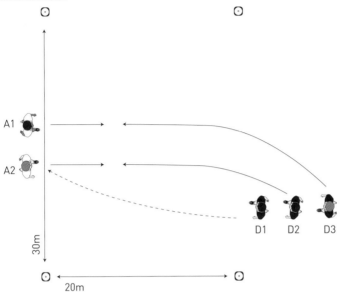

Objective: To develop communication and coordination in players chasing attacking kicks.

Equipment: Four cones, lots of players and balls in a 30 m x 20 m grid.

Description: Defenders 1–3 stand at one end of the grid, one behind each other. Attackers 1 and 2 (A1 and A2) set up to receive a kick at the other end of the grid. D1 kicks deep to A1 or A2 who catches, and then they set off up the grid as if counter-attacking. It is the job of D2 and D3 to defend. Players rotate roles frequently to avoid fatigue.

Coaching points: It is vital that the chasing players work together. If one runs up too quickly he will leave a gap that the attackers can exploit. One player running up on their own is easily beaten by a stationary player. Encourage the defenders to be aware of where their partner is while the ball is in the air. Indeed, after an initial 'spot' a runner can gauge where a ball will land and can therefore afford a look around to see where supporting runners and defenders are. If the kick is high and the catcher is isolated (and therefore unlikely to pass), both defending players should stay close together. If the kick is caught early and other counterattackers are in support, the chasers must communicate to mark both ball carrier and supporting chasers. Chaser/runners must be behind the ball when it is kicked.

Progression: Start with two groups of defenders, each with a number 1–4. A designated player kicks the ball and the coach calls random numbers '1s' or '3s' etc., so that the players have to react and form up quickly to chase and defend.

England's Toby Flood practising his kicking techniques.

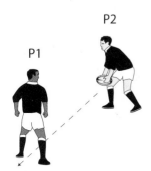

Objective: To introduce the skills required to smother and gather a rolling ball.

Equipment: One ball per pair.

Description: Divide the players into pairs. Player 1 (P1) stands with their legs shoulder-width apart, and player 2 (P2) stands 1 m in front of P1 with the ball. P2 rolls the ball through the legs of P1 – no more than 5 m. P2 runs forward around P1 and falls on the ball to gather it, recovers quickly and then returns the ball to P1 at which point the roles are reversed and the drill continues.

Coaching points: P2 should aim to fall slightly in front of the ball and slide onto it. The objective is to make the whole body into a 'net' to smother the ball as it bounces rather than to try and simply drop straight down onto the ball. Start slowly so that the process is clearly understood before speeding up the drill.

Progression: Make sure that P2 practises falling on to both left and right sides by making the initial run past alternating shoulders of P1. As competence grows the players can experiment by rolling the ball out at different angles and increasing the approach speed. They will soon discover that the harder they fall on the ball the easier it is to use their momentum to regain their feet.

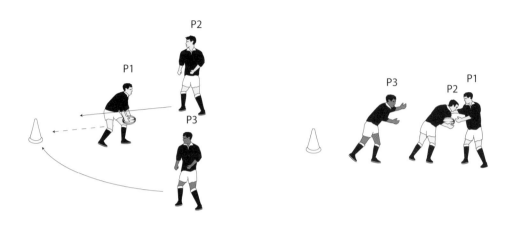

Objective: To develop defensive skills required to smother and gather a rolling ball; to challenge decision-making and communication in a defensive environment.

Equipment: One ball for every three players.

Description: Player 1 (P1) stands with legs shoulder-width apart with the ball. Players 2 and 3 (P2 and P3) stand 1 m in front of player 1. P1 calls out a number (to identify P2 or P3) and immediately rolls the ball backwards through his own legs – no more than 10 m. P2 and P3 run through and the designated player falls on the ball to gather it, recovers quickly and then drives into P1, allowing the supporting player to form a mini-maul to protect the ball. When the ball is well secured the coach halts the drill and the players rotate.

Coaching points: Start slowly so that the process is clearly understood before speeding up the drill. As the drill seeks to replicate a defensive situation the supporting player must work hard to get around the player gathering the ball so that he is in an onside position, joining the mini-maul from behind the ball gatherer.

Progression: Once the roles are clear to all players, remove the initial call from P1 and ask the runners to decide who is best positioned to fall on the ball based on where it rolls and make a loud, clear and early call.

receiving the kick off – unopposed drill

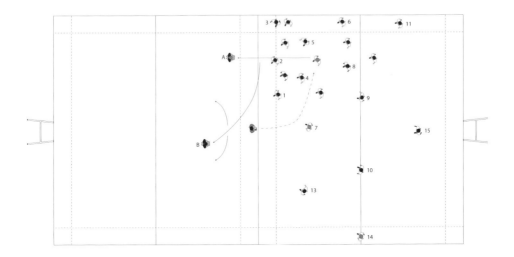

Objective: To provide opportunities for players to practise restart skills in a game situation.

Equipment: A full XV of players, plus two extra players, two tackle shields, a full pitch and one ball.

Description: The drill begins at the halfway line. Players are set out as shown in the illustration. The coach kicks off with a drop kick to the forwards. A player gathers the ball, makes ground and passes to a team member. Further ground is made into tackle shield (A) and the player goes to ground. A ruck is formed and the ball is played back to the scrum-half. Two passes are made to the inside centre. The centre makes ground into tackle shield (B) and goes to ground. A second ruck and the ball goes through all hands out to the wing. Drill stopped and repeated two or three times. Change the tackle shield carriers.

Coaching points: Facing the kick off, players must ensure that all spaces are covered. The front row stands on the 10 m line about 5 m apart. The remainder of the forwards take up scrum positions at distances of 5 m from each other. It is easier to be further back from the kick off and have to run forwards, rather than be too close and have the ball go over their heads. For the purposes of this early drill, if the ball does not cross the 10 m line it is not in play.

Progression: Instead of a ruck at the shields, players stay on their feet to form a maul.

drill 92   making the kick off – unopposed drill

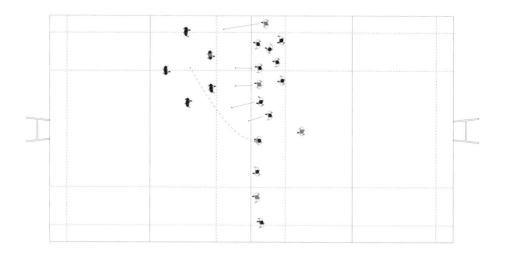

Objective: To provide opportunities for players to practise restart skills in a game situation.

Equipment: A full XV of players, plus three to six extra players and one ball.

Description: Use a full pitch for this drill, and play begins at the halfway line. Players are set out as shown in the illustration. A designated player kicks off with a drop kick. The three opposition players attempt to field the ball. The attacking side follows up the kick, and tag tackles the opposition.

Coaching points: The attacking forwards must stay behind the kicker at all times, otherwise they are offside. The kicker must make the ball cross the 10 m line. An ideal kick is high enough to give time for the chasing forwards to arrive as the ball comes down. It is important for the kicker to have good skills with the drop kick. Forwards should start behind the kicker to generate speed. Encourage the backs to come up in a line abreast alongside the advancing forwards to block any movement across the pitch from defenders. Repeat the exercise, changing players and kickers.

Progression: The two drills of 'making a kick off' and 'receiving a kick off' can be combined into an opposed drill. Divide the forwards up into two equal groups. The defending side receives the kick off in the face of the advancing attackers and forms either a ruck or maul. The drill can end at this point. The basic objective of the drill is for people to know what to do at the kick off.

drill 93

making and receiving the kick off at the 22 m line – unopposed

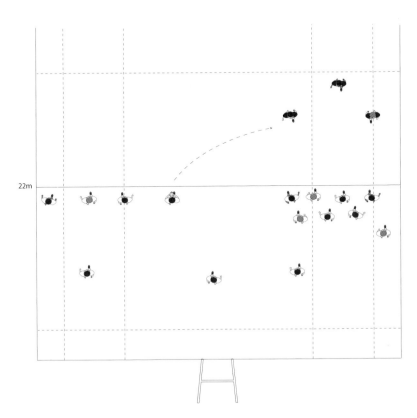

22m

Objective: To provide opportunities for players to practise restart skills from the 22m line in a game situation.

Equipment: A full XV of players plus three extra players, a full pitch and one ball.

Description: Play begins at the 22 m line. Players are set out as shown in the illustration. A designated player kicks off with a drop kick. The three opposition players attempt to field the ball. The attacking side follows up the kick and tag tackles the opposition.

Coaching points: The ball simply has to cross the 22 m line to be in play. Players must stay behind the kicker. The height of the kick is again important to provide time for the chasers. Repeat several times with changes of kickers.

Progression: Divide the players into two groups to practise opposed 22 m restarts.

defensive clearing kicks from the 5 m line

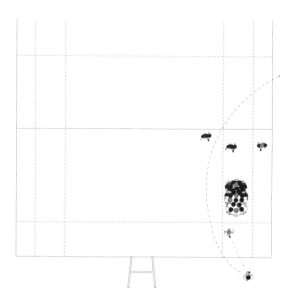

Objective: To develop drills and skills to operate defensive kicking ability from behind the 5 m line, in the goal area or any defensive position within the 22 m area.

Equipment: One ball.

Description: Divide the players into two sets of forwards, a scrum-half, a kicker and a ball, plus 2–3 defending players. Set an uncontested scrum 5 m from any line that replicates the try line and close to the touchline. The defending side puts in the ball, which is heeled, unopposed. The ball is then delivered to a player standing some 5–8 m directly behind the scrum. He kicks to touch. Players from the opposition scrum attempt to tackle the kicker or charge down the kick. Alternate the forwards to be defending and experiment with kickers.

Coaching points: Communication between the scrum-half and the kicker is vital to ensure each is aware of the other's position. The scrum-half's pass must be flat and accurate to give the kicker time. The kicker should stand at the extremity of the scrum-half's pass to maximise time available for the kick. If the kicker drops the ball he must touch it down immediately. The defending scrum-half should encourage his scrum/maul to put on a push to drive back the opposition. This will keep loose forwards tied down to restrict the push rather than ready to charge the kick.

Progression: Set an uncontested lineout on the 5 m line. The ball is caught, protected with a maul, and then smuggled back to the scrum-half, passed to the kicker, who finds touch.

CONTROLLED
GAMES

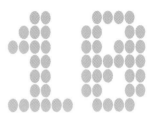

These drills cover typical game situations and introduce some basic tactics of rugby to players with some understanding of the game and who need to develop their skills. The drills will give players some experience of coping with different scenarios, trying out different options and developing their decision-making skills.

Aim to keep the practices simple at the start; try to limit the number of things you are asking players to remember. Encourage them to try out different positions to help them understand the roles and responsibilities of each position and decide which position they prefer or are better suited to through experience. This also helps develop good team spirit!

Young players not only have to learn the basic skills of rugby (control, passing, catching and kicking techniques, tackling, etc.), but they also have to learn the roles and responsibilities of the team positions and be able to understand them sufficiently to put all this into practice in a game. This is a challenge even for players who have played some rugby and they will need lots of support, encouragement and praise to help them develop these skills.

There can be a tendency for players to revert back to old habits when playing in a game rather than try newly coached skills or techniques, even if you have just delivered a highly successful coaching session incorporating well-structured drills! Conditioned games and scenarios provide an opportunity for players and coaches to put the new skills and techniques into practice in a game situation. For this to be fully effective the coach must make sure that the objective and the link between the drill and the game are very clear and understood – ask the players to help make this link. Without this understanding there is a tendency for a conditioned game to turn into a run-around with lots of frustration.

When players are under pressure, faced with defenders and an impending tackle, the easy, safe option is often to hurl the ball any which way and get rid of it – or run away with no thought to attacking lines. The drills they have just run through are long forgotten.

Enthusiasm can often get the better of players, too, with everyone running after the ball shouting at team-mates, with little regard for form, organisation or communication on the field.

To encourage players (of all ages and abilities!) to practise using the skills you have drilled during coaching sessions in a game situation, it sometimes helps to make the new skill or technique a condition in the game, with failure to use or apply this rule resulting in a free kick or penalty to the opponents.

The following drills are suggestions for conditioned games and scenarios to help younger, inexperienced players develop their rugby skills and improve their confidence on the field.

Coaching points

1 Link the condition in the game to the drills that have been practiced as part of the training session – the idea is to encourage players to try out their new skills.
2 Only apply one condition at a time for young players – don't give them too much extra to think about, as this will only confuse things.
3 Use conditioned games for a short time to avoid frustration building when trying to learn something new.
4 Encourage players to spot when the skills and techniques have been used, too – this is useful for players waiting to join in with the game and for players on the field. Extra points can be awarded if the team spots when the condition has been correctly applied.

The Australian Wallabies during a training session practising defensive tactics to stop attacking play.

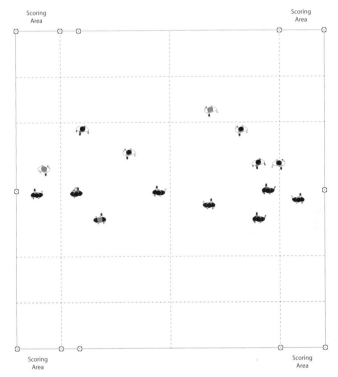

Objective: To provide opportunities for players to practise specific skills in a contested game environment.

This game is to practise tackling, running and passing and moving the ball away into space creating room for runners.

Equipment: Eight cones and one ball.

Description: On a pitch (no more than half a full pitch), use the cones to mark out the corners and halfway line. Divide the players into two teams of 8–10. The game is played under the full rules of rugby but all infringements plus the ball off the pitch are dealt with by a 'tap' penalty. Kicking is not allowed. The opposition retires 7 m for all restarts. Additional rules are as follows:

- each try is worth 3 points.
- a penalty is awarded for running backwards or across the pitch and running the ball back into congested spaces.
- the strongest runners are not allowed to dominate play. After scoring once they can be awarded a point for every break they make and pass that leads to a try.

Progression: At the corners add a second cone 3 m in from the corner cone. This becomes the only scoring area on the goal line. Strong emphasis is placed on moving the ball wide and not running wide.

drill 96   the whole game situation – unopposed

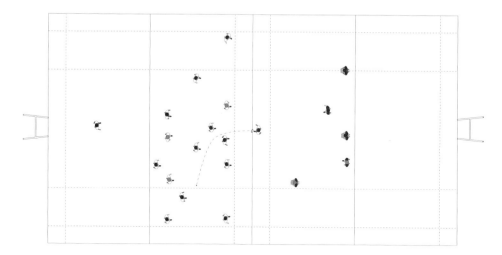

Objective: To accustom young players to the constantly changing structure of the game.

Equipment: A full XV of players plus four to five extra players, two to three tackle shields and one ball.

Description: Use a full pitch for this drill. Begin with the XV receiving kick off. Spare players offer some token opposition, particularly at lineouts and kick offs. They can carry the tackle shields as and when needed. Players should play as if they have opponents, but the coach uses commands to structure the proceedings:

- **'set'** – the ball carrier turns, as if tackled, and remains on his feet. Forwards maul and smuggle the ball to the scrum-half then out to a backs passing movement.
- **'tackle'** – the ball carrier goes to ground. Forwards ruck ball to scrum-half, to backs or to late arriving forwards.
- **'blind'** – for the scrum-half to go blind.
- **'link'** – ball carrier to link with nearest player.
- **'wide'** – ball to be passed to wings.

With imagination a whole game can be created. The coach can award penalties, defensive and attacking lineouts and scrums, 22 restarts and halfway restarts.

Coaching points: The emphasis must be on support play. Players are not allowed to run too far. Late arriving players at a ruck must decide whether they are needed. If the ball is already won they can hang back to support the three quarters. Discourage forwards 'loitering' between 9 and 10. The correct position is either in front or behind this line so that the scrum-half can choose to release the ball to the backs.

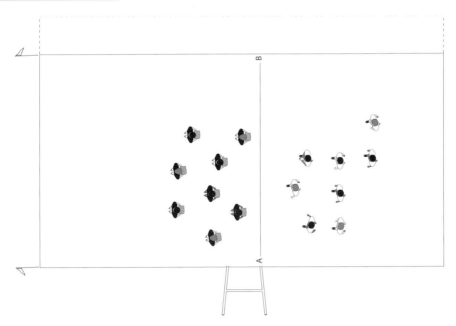

Objective: To accustom players to close-quarter skills required for effective mauling.

Equipment: Eight tackle shields and one ball.

Description: Divide the players into eight attackers, and eight defenders with tackle shields. Set up in a restricted area approximately 10 m x 15 m. The dead ball area is ideal for this drill. The attacking team starts with the ball on line AB, and the defenders with shields stand 2 m in front. On the coach's command, the attacking team runs out and sets up a maul against the pads. The objective is to get the ball to the other end of the grid to 'score'. The rules are as in a game (offside, collapsing, etc.); the only other addition is that the ball cannot be passed, only transferred or smuggled, between players. Defenders must try and force the maul backwards to keep them away from their try-line.

Coaching points: The emphasis must be on correct mauling technique. As there are no defenders competing for the ball there will be little disruption other than the pads forcing the maul back. As in a real game, the coach can stop the drill if the ball becomes locked, or is stopped. If the maul goes to ground the ball must be presented quickly for the next attacker to pick and drive to set up another maul. This can be a very intensive drill and competition is to be encouraged. Remember that you are dealing with young players and allow plenty of rest to ensure that good technique is being practised.

Progression: Dispense with pads and play games with equal sides – full contact.

WARMING DOWN

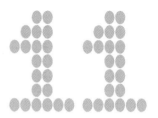

This tends to be a much-ignored area of coaching sessions and as mentioned before, the warm-down is the place to work on flexibility. Children have a natural flexibility and while muscle fatigue and stiffness is not likely to be a major issue for the younger player, awareness of warming down is a good habit to get them into.

If stretches are carried out consistently during a warm-down this can prevent muscle stiffness and soreness in the days following matches, which is more important for older players.

Structure the warm-down to target any specific areas of the body that have been worked during the session, i.e. if you have included lots of speed drills make sure the warm-down includes some stretches for the legs (such as calf and hamstring stretches).

The great benefit of a structured warm-down is that it provides the coach with quiet time at the end of the session to reflect on the aims of the session and what has been achieved. Players can contribute to this reflection, which helps with their understanding and development of the skills. It also gives the coach a chance to remind players of any important news or information – rather than players disappearing in a mad dash at the end of a session and missing out hearing the next match details!

Lee Byrne, Shane Williams and James Hook performing dynamic stretches at the end of a Wales training session.

drill 98 hamstring reach

Objective: To warm down the body and improve flexibility.

Equipment: One ball per player.

Description: Line the players up along the touchline with feet wider than shoulder-width apart and the ball between their feet. On the coach's command, the players reach down (keeping their legs straight at all times), pick up the ball and place it as far back through their legs as they can. The players then walk backwards until their feet are in line with the ball and repeat the drill. The aim is to cover the given distance (approximately 10 m) in as few pick-ups as possible.

Coaching points: Watch for cheats who bend their legs to gain an advantage! Remind players that this is a slow, controlled race and that form is everything.

drill 99 side stretch

Objective: To warm down the body and improve flexibility.

Equipment: One ball per player.

Description: Line the players up with their right side facing into a 5 m grid, feet wider than shoulder-width apart, legs straight and the ball in front of their left foot. On the coach's command, the players bend down (keeping their legs straight), pick up the ball and place it in front of their right foot. Then, leaving the ball where it is, the players swap feet, progressing into the grid, so that the ball is by their left foot once more. The movement is then repeated for a set distance – 10 m is more than enough for this drill.

Coaching points: Watch for cheats who bend their legs or pick up with one hand to gain an advantage!

drill 100 circle stretch 1

Objective: To warm down the body and improve flexibility.

Equipment: One ball between six players.

Description: Ask the players to form a circle with their feet wider than shoulder-width apart, and their feet touching those of the next players (i.e. right foot to left foot). Keeping their legs straight, all the players reach down and hang their hands as close to the floor as possible. The ball is rolled from one player to another around the circle. After ten passes in total, walk the players around for a minute, then repeat. A football can be used for easier rolling.

Coaching points: Watch for cheats who are bending their legs to gain an advantage!

Progression: If you have enough players, form two or more groups and race them to see who is first to complete the passes.

Objective: To warm down the body and improve flexibility.

Equipment: One ball between six players.

Description: Ask players to sit back-to-back in a circle with their legs wide apart and feet touching. The ball is passed in order around the circle. Each player must give and take the ball with two hands every time.

Coaching points: This drill provides a stretch to the backs of the legs and requires good flexibility, as each player must rotate their trunk to make the pass. If players lack flexibility, they will creep their bottoms away from the group so that they are leaning back rather than sitting upright. Try and keep the legs nice and straight throughout.

Progression: If you have enough players, form two or more groups and race the first to complete the passes. Vary the direction of passing on command.

Fun for everyone – school children playing rugby.